Sunset
Pies & Pastries
—STEP-BY-STEP TECHNIQUES—

By the Editors of Sunset Books
and Sunset Magazine

Lane Publishing Co. • Menlo Park, California

As easy as pie...

...or quiche, or cream puffs or croissants. Making marvelous pies and pastries is simple when you know how. And this book gives you the help you'll need—step-by-step photographs and illustrations of basic techniques, along with dozens of great recipes.

You'll find traditional favorites—tempting fruit pies and cobblers, delicate tartlets, sinfully rich cheesecakes—as well as elegant chou paste and puff pastry creations. But our selections aren't limited just to desserts. We've included coffeecakes for breakfast or brunch, quiches for lunch, savory appetizer tidbits, and pastry-wrapped entrées suitable for dinner.

For their generosity in sharing props for use in our photographs, we're grateful to Fillamento, Forrest Jones, Sue Fisher King, Jan Platt, Set Your Table, La Ville du Soleil, and Williams-Sonoma Kitchenware. We also extend special thanks to Rebecca LaBrum for her thorough and thoughtful editing of the manuscript.

Coordinating Editor
Linda J. Selden

Research & Text
Elaine R. Woodard
Janeth Johnson Nix
Cynthia Scheer
Elizabeth Friedman

Design
Lea Damiano Phelps
Kathy Avanzino Barone

Illustrations
Sally Shimizu

Photography
Darrow M. Watt

Photo Stylists
Elizabeth Ross
Lynne B. Morrall

Cover: Homey and old-fashioned, or pastry-shop fancy? With pies and pastries, you can have both, as the examples on our cover show. Deep-dish Blueberry Pie (page 23) brims with bright, juicy berries. The elegant Cream Puffs (page 71) are filled with pastry cream and dusted with powdered sugar. Photography by Darrow M. Watt. Cover design by Elizabeth Ross.

Editor, Sunset Books: David E. Clark
First printing September 1985
Second printing March 1986

Contents

Apple pie à la mode—that's one dessert that never goes out of style! The recipe is on page 16.

Special Features

Pie Crusts

A good crust is the start of a great pie. And in this chapter, you'll find quite a selection of good beginnings—flaky pastry shells, eight flavors of crunchy crumb crusts, even a few specialty pastries. In addition to recipes, we provide step-by-step instructions, backed up by photographs and illustrations, for mixing, rolling, and shaping pie crusts.

Getting your pie off to a perfect start requires something more than good technique, though; the right pan is important as well. For best results, *always use the pan the recipe specifies.*

Pie pans. Standard pie pans range from 8 to 10 inches in diameter, 1 to 1½ inches in depth. Our recipes usually call for 9 or 10-inch pans; to measure a pan, place a ruler across the top and check the distance from one inner rim to the other.

A few recipes specify 1½-inch-deep pans. If the recipe requests this depth, don't use a shallower pan or the filling will overflow. (If you don't have a pan that's 1½ inches deep, you'll need to bake part of the filling separately.)

For an evenly browned crust, choose non-shiny pie pans—those made from tin, porcelain, aluminum, anodized aluminum, or heatproof glass. All these materials absorb heat rather than reflect it, helping the crust to brown. Avoid pans with a nonstick finish; crusts baked in these tend to turn out pale and soggy.

Heatproof glass has one advantage over the other materials mentioned above because it's transparent: since you can see the crust through the pan, you can easily tell when it's fully baked. *When using heatproof glass pans, reduce oven temperature specified in recipe by 25 degrees.*

Spring-form pans. These are round metal pans, usually about 2½ inches deep, ranging from 8 to 12 inches in diameter (our recipes usually call for 9 or 10-inch pans). The sides are held in place by a clamp; when you loosen the clamp, the sides spring open and can be removed. This type of pan is especially popular for cheesecakes, and in fact is often called a "cheesecake pan."

Tart pans. These metal pans are made in two parts: a fluted or rippled ring that forms the sides, and a removable bottom. To remove a baked tart from its pan, you simply push up on the pan bottom. Tart pans are shallow (usually about 1 inch deep), ranging from 6 to 12 inches in diameter.

Tartlet pans. Ranging in size from about 2 inches to 4 inches, tartlet pans are available in a variety of shapes. Some look like miniature pie pans; others are shaped like hearts, flowers, or stars. *Barquette pans* (see photo, page 46) are a special type of tartlet pan—they're oval, with pointed tips and ridged or pointed sides.

If you don't own tartlet pans, you can form tartlet shells by draping the pastry over the backs of muffin cups.

Short Pastry

Describe a pie crust or cookie as "short," and any cook will know just what you mean: something rich, often buttery, with a crisp, flaky, tender texture. But the word "short" really refers to the structural properties that give a baked good those characteristics. The fat in short pastries coats and separates the strands of gluten in the flour, actually making them shorter and preventing them from clinging together. Hence the reason why "shortening" is a common generic term for fats. And hence the flaky, melt-in-the-mouth quality of short pastry—as opposed to the chewy, springy texture of yeast breads, in which the flour's gluten strands are long and well developed.

There are 2 basic types of short pastry: *sweetened and unsweetened*. Unsweetened short pastry is made from flour, salt, liquid, and fat. It's very flaky, with just enough structure to hold a filling, but not enough to be lifted whole from the baking pan. For this reason, it's typically used for pies and pastries to be served, a piece at a time, right out of their baking containers.

Sweetened short crusts are more crisp than flaky; they're made with flour, egg, sugar, and butter or margarine. These crusts are popular for tarts and for pies made in spring-form pans, since they're sturdy enough to stand on their own when removed from a baking pan.

Whether sweetened or unsweetened, a good short crust should have a rich golden brown color after baking; its surface should look flaky or slightly blistery, not compact and smooth. The texture should be tender, so the crust cuts easily with a fork. To achieve such perfect pastry, be sure to follow exactly our directions for mixing, rolling, and shaping (see pages 6, 7, 8, 12, and 13). It's helpful, too, to know something about the ingredients that go into short pastry.

Basic Ingredients

What kind of flour is best for short pastry? How do different types of fats affect the texture of a crust? You'll find the answers below, along with pointers on measuring flour and shortening.

Fat. More than any other basic ingredient, the type of fat determines the characteristics of the baked pastry. For unsweetened pastry, many people prefer *lard*: it's pliable and easy to work with, and has great shortening power. *Solid vegetable shortening* is also easily worked, but has less shortening power. Nonetheless, it too produces a tender, flaky crust, and is favored by those who object to the fla-

vor of lard or who wish to avoid animal fats. *Butter* has still less shortening power than solid shortening. Used as the sole fat in an unsweetened (eggless) pastry, it produces a dough that's hard to work with and a brittle baked crust. If you want the flavor of butter in your unsweetened pastry, use a blend of solid shortening and butter—you'll get a short, flaky crust. (It's best not to substitute margarine for butter in unsweetened pastry; the result will be crumbly, not flaky.)

Butter or margarine is used in sweetened short pastries. In combination with sugar and egg, either fat makes a crisp, sturdy crust that's ideal for tarts and tartlets.

Vegetable oil produces an easily worked dough and a baked crust that's mealy rather than flaky. Because oil pastry has little porosity, it's a good choice for very liquid fillings. Use corn or safflower oil for this type of pastry; avoid peanut oil, which gives crusts a pronounced flavor.

Whatever fat you use, measure it accurately; too much fat makes a greasy, crumbly crust. Pack solid shortening or lard into a dry measure; run a spatula through fat to eliminate air pockets, then level off with a straightedge. Measure oil at eye level in a liquid measure. *For best results, have fat as cold as possible.*

Flour. Use all-purpose flour for pie crusts. Bread flour makes a tough pastry; cake or pastry flour produces too fragile a crust. To measure flour, gently spoon it into a dry measure and level off the top with a straightedge. Never pack or shake down flour in the cup; excess flour in the dough makes for tough, hard pastry.

Salt & spices. Salt and spices both bring out the crust's flavor. Spices also give pastry a special aroma, and can enhance the flavor of the filling.

Sugar. Granulated sugar goes into sweetened short crusts. This ingredient makes the pastry sturdier; it also caramelizes during baking, giving the crust a rich brown color.

Liquid. Some type of liquid—water, milk, fruit juice—is used in almost all unsweetened short crusts. *Always have liquid as cold as possible*; if it's warm or hot, it will melt the fat in the dough and make the crust less flaky. It's also important to add just enough liquid to hold the dough together. Too much liquid makes a sticky, glutinous dough and a tough baked crust.

Egg. Pastry made with whole egg or egg yolks is extra crisp and rich tasting. It's also sturdier and less likely to become soggy than pastry made without egg. *Use eggs straight from the refrigerator;* lightly beat before adding.

Mixing, Rolling & Shaping the Crust

1 With a pastry blender or 2 knives, cut shortening into flour mixture until particles are about the size of small peas.

2 Place chilled dough round on a lightly floured board. Place rolling pin in center of dough and roll from center to edge with even, light strokes. Work quickly and handle dough as little as possible.

3 After unrolling dough from pin (see photo 5), ease pastry into ungreased pan. Work out from center, using fingertips to fit dough over bottom and up sides of pan. Trim, leaving a ½-inch overhang.

4 For a single-crust pie, fold overhang under, making pastry even with pan rim. Place one thumb on inside edge; place other thumb and index finger on outside. Pinch pastry around inside thumb to flute edge.

5 For a double-crust pie, roll out second dough round to same size circle as first; wrap loosely around rolling pin, lift onto filling, and gently unroll to cover. Trim, leaving a 1-inch overhang.

6 Fold edges of top crust under edges of bottom crust. Place one index finger on outside edge, thumb and other index finger on inside edge. Pinch pastry around outside finger to flute edge. Cut steam vents.

6 Pie Crusts

UNSWEETENED SHORT CRUSTS

Type of Crust & Yield*	Flour	Salt	Other Ingredients	Fat	Cold Water
Flaky Pastry 9" single crust	1 cup plus 2 table-spoons	¼ teaspoon		6 tablespoons solid vegetable shortening or lard *or* ¼ cup solid vegetable shortening plus 2 tablespoons butter	3–4 tablespoons
9" double crust or 10" single crust	2¼ cups	½ teaspoon		¾ cup solid vegetable shortening or lard *or* ½ cup solid vegetable shortening plus ¼ cup butter	6–8 tablespoons
Cheddar Cheese Pastry 9" single crust	1 cup	¼ teaspoon	½ cup finely shredded sharp Cheddar cheese	¼ cup solid vegetable shortening	3–4 tablespoons
Flaky Butter Pastry 9" single crust	1 cup	¼ teaspoon	1 egg, lightly beaten	6 tablespoons butter	
Nutty Short Pastry 9" single crust	1 cup	⅛ teaspoon	⅓ cup finely ground almonds, pecans, or walnuts	¼ cup butter plus 2 tablespoons solid vegetable shortening	2–3 tablespoons
Oatmeal Pastry 9" single crust	1 cup		⅓ cup regular or quick-cooking rolled oats	7 tablespoons butter or margarine	2–3 tablespoons
Seasoned Pastry 9" double crust	2¼ cups	½ teaspoon	½ teaspoon ground allspice, caraway seeds, or chili powder *or* 2 tablespoons parsley flakes *or* ¼ teaspoon dill weed	¾ cup solid vegetable shortening or lard	6–8 tablespoons

*Recipe for oil pastry (9" double crust) is on page 8.

Mixing the Pastry Dough

Stir together flour, salt, and other dry ingredients (if used). Cut butter or margarine (if used) into chunks; then, with a pastry blender or 2 knives, cut in all fat until particles are about the size of small peas. If using a butter-shortening combination, cut in butter first, then shortening. (Since solid shortening is softer than butter, it would be overworked if both fats were cut into flour at the same time.)

Pour the minimum amount of water listed into a cup. Stirring flour mixture lightly and quickly with a fork, sprinkle water over mixture, a tablespoon at a time, stirring just until all flour is moistened. (For Flaky Butter Pastry, pour in egg all at once.) If mixture seems dry or crumbly, sprinkle with just 1 more tablespoon water; dough should not be damp or sticky. Stir in a circular motion, scraping bowl bottom with fork, until dough clings together and almost cleans sides of bowl.

With your hands, gather dough into a ball; if you're making a double-crust pie, divide ball into 2 portions, one slightly larger than the other. Flatten each ball into a 4-inch round, wrap in plastic wrap, and refrigerate for 1 hour. (This resting time is important—it gives flour a chance to absorb liquid ingredients, tenderizing the dough and making it easier to handle.)

Roll out and shape chilled dough as directed on facing page and on pages 12 and 13.

Oil Pastry

This unsweetened short pastry uses liquid fat instead of solid shortening. Be sure to roll out this pastry immediately after mixing. Oil absorbs flour quickly and tends to blend completely with it; if you let the dough stand, the crust will be tough and greasy. This recipe makes a 9-inch double crust.

> 2¼ cups all-purpose flour
> 1 teaspoon salt
> ⅔ cup vegetable oil
> ¼ cup cold water

In a bowl, stir together flour and salt. In another bowl, combine oil and water. Beat with a wire whisk until creamy, then pour into flour mixture, stirring with a fork until dough holds together.

With your hands, gather dough into a ball; divide into 2 portions, one slightly larger than the other. Immediately roll out larger portion to an 11-inch circle between two 12-inch squares of wax paper. Peel off top paper. Place pastry in pan, paper side up; peel off paper, then ease pastry into pan. Trim overhang to ½ inch. Roll out remaining portion of dough to an 11-inch circle between two squares of wax paper; peel off top paper. Spoon filling into shell. Place remaining dough circle on pie, paper side up; peel off paper. Form a decorative edge as directed on pages 12 and 13.

For a 9-inch single crust, prepare ½ recipe Oil Pastry as directed above; fit pastry into pan as directed above. Form a decorative edge.

SWEETENED SHORT CRUSTS

Type of Crust & Yield	Flour	Granulated Sugar	Other Ingredients	Butter or Margarine	Egg
Sweet Butter Pastry 9" single crust or 10" tart crust	1 cup	2 tablespoons		6 tablespoons butter	2 egg yolks or 1 whole egg
11" tart crust or 10" spring-form crust	1⅓ cups	¼ cup		½ cup (¼ lb.) butter	1 whole egg
10 x 15" baking pan	2 cups	¼ cup		¾ cup (¼ lb. plus ¼ cup) butter	2 egg yolks or 1 whole egg
Almond Pastry 11" tart crust or 10" spring-form crust	1 cup	¼ cup	⅓ cup finely ground almonds and ½ teaspoon grated lemon peel	½ cup (¼ lb.) butter or margarine	2 egg yolks or 1 whole egg
Lemon or Orange Pastry 11" tart crust	1⅓ cups	¼ cup	1 teaspoon grated lemon or orange peel	½ cup (¼ lb.) butter	1 whole egg
Sweet Oatmeal Pastry 10" or 11" tart crust	⅔ cup	½ cup	1 cup regular or quick-cooking rolled oats	¾ cup (¼ lb. plus ¼ cup) butter or margarine	1 egg yolk

Mixing the Pastry Dough

In a bowl, stir together flour, sugar, and other dry ingredients (if used). Cut butter or margarine into chunks and add to flour mixture; stir to coat. With a pastry blender or 2 knives, cut butter into flour until fine particles form. Add egg and stir with a fork until dough clings together. With your hands, gather dough into a ball; wrap in plastic wrap and refrigerate for 1 hour.

Roll out and shape chilled dough as shown on page 6 and as directed on pages 12 and 13; or simply press firmly and evenly over bottom and up sides of pan.

Crumb Crusts

Quick, easy crumb crusts make delicious nests to cradle chiffon pie fillings; they're just as good for freezer pies and cheesecakes. Whatever filling you choose, make sure it's fairly thick—if it's too juicy or wet, it will cause the crumbs to disintegrate, and you'll end up with a soggy crust that falls apart when cut.

Though crumb crusts need not be baked before they're filled, we prefer to bake ours. A baked crust holds its shape better, is less likely to become soggy, and cuts into neat wedges without crumbling. It has a toastier flavor, too.

Each of the eight crusts below will line a 1½-inch-deep 9-inch pie pan or a 9 or 10-inch spring-form pan. To make the fine crumbs required, break the crackers or cookies into pieces, then whirl to fine crumbs in a blender or food processor. Or place crackers or cookies in a plastic bag and finely crush with a rolling pin.

Mixing & Shaping the Crust

Preheat oven to proper temperature (see chart below). In a bowl, combine crumbs, sugar (if used), and other ingredients (if used); stir in butter. Press mixture firmly over bottom and sides of an ungreased 9-inch pie pan or a buttered 9 or 10-inch spring-form pan. (If desired, press crumbs over bottom only of a spring-form pan.) For a more evenly shaped pie crust, distribute crumbs in pan; then press another pie pan of the same size into crumb-filled pan until crust is of uniform thickness. Lift off top pan. Bake crust (see below for baking time), then let cool on a rack before filling.

CRUMB CRUSTS

Type of Crust	Fine Crumbs	Granulated Sugar	Other Ingredients	Melted Butter or Margarine	Baking Temperature	Baking Time
Chocolate	1½ cups (30 2¼" chocolate cookie wafers)			⅓ cup	350°	8 minutes
Chocolate-Peanut	1 cup (20 2¼" chocolate cookie wafers)		⅓ cup finely chopped peanuts	⅓ cup	350°	8 minutes
Gingersnap	1½ cups (27 2¼" ginger-snap cookies)			⅓ cup	350°	8 minutes
Graham Cracker	1½ cups (24 graham cracker squares)	¼ cup		⅓ cup	350°	10 minutes
Nutty Graham	1¼ cups (20 graham cracker squares)	2 table-spoons	¼ cup finely chopped almonds, pecans, or walnuts	⅓ cup	325°	8 minutes
Macaroon	1½ cups (12 2½" crisp coconut maca-roon cookies)			¼ cup	350°	8 minutes
Vanilla	1½ cups (36 1½" vanilla cookie wafers)			⅓ cup	350°	10 minutes
Zwieback	1½ cups (20 zwieback toast slices)	¼ cup		⅓ cup	350°	10 minutes

Specialty Crusts

To make basic short pastry (see pages 7 and 8), you combine all the dry ingredients, then cut in solid fat with a pastry blender or 2 knives. But different techniques are used to mix the three short pastries on this page: a rich cream cheese pastry, a sweet chocolate-nut crust, and a quick processor pastry. (For a sweetened cream cheese pastry, see our recipe for *kolache* on page 55.)

Cream Cheese Pastry

(9-inch double crust or 10-inch single crust)

This versatile pastry is suitable for a variety of fillings, both sweet and savory. You can make and refrigerate the dough a day in advance; before rolling, let it stand at room temperature just until pliable (dough should not actually reach room temperature).

    1 large package (8 oz.) cream cheese, softened
    1 cup (½ lb.) butter or margarine, softened
    ¼ teaspoon salt
    2 cups all-purpose flour

In a bowl, beat cream cheese and butter until smooth; beat in salt. Slowly stir in flour to make a stiff dough.

Turn dough out of bowl onto a piece of plastic wrap; pull up corners of plastic to enclose dough, shaping it into a 4-inch-wide round. Refrigerate for at least 4 hours or up to 24 hours.

For rolling, shaping, and baking blind, follow directions on pages 12 and 13.

Chocolate-Nut Crust

(9-inch single crust)

Chocolate lovers will rave about this chocolaty, nutty crust. It's an especially good choice for Irish Coffee Pie (page 40) and Chocolate Cream Pie (page 34).

    1 cup all-purpose flour
    ¼ cup firmly packed brown sugar
    ¾ cup finely chopped nuts
    1 ounce semisweet chocolate, grated
    ⅓ cup butter or margarine, melted

Preheat oven to 375°. In a bowl, combine flour, sugar, nuts, and chocolate. With a fork, stir in butter just until dry ingredients are moistened. Press mixture over bottom and up sides of a 9-inch pie pan. Lightly prick all over with a fork.

Bake for 15 minutes; place on a rack and let cool completely before filling.

Rich Processor Pie Pastry

(9-inch single crust)

If you have a food processor, you can use it to mix just about any kind of crust in seconds—the step-by-step photos on the facing page show how to make sweetened short pastry and crumb crusts in the processor.

For an unsweetened processor pastry, try the recipe below. The dough is easy to roll out; the baked crust is flaky and tender, with a delicious flavor. Use it for any pie or quiche, or as a wrapping for hors d'oeuvre turnovers.

Because the food processor works so rapidly, it's important to start with frozen shortening and cold, firm butter. Cold fat will remain in particles (crucial for flakiness) when processed, rather than be creamed.

    1¼ cups all-purpose flour
    ¼   teaspoon salt
    ¼   cup *frozen* solid vegetable shortening
         (remove from measuring cup before
         freezing)
    ¼   cup *firm* butter
    3   tablespoons ice water

Insert metal blade in processor work bowl; add flour and salt. Cut shortening and butter into ½-inch chunks and distribute over flour mixture. Process until fat particles are the size of small peas. With motor running, pour ice water slowly through feed tube. Turn off motor. Mixture will still look crumbly; don't allow it to form a ball. (If dough accidentally forms a ball, you can still use it, but pastry made from overprocessed dough won't be as flaky.)

Turn dough out onto a piece of plastic wrap; pull up corners to enclose dough, shaping it into a 4-inch-wide round. Refrigerate for 1 hour. (This resting time is important; it makes dough easier to handle and more tender. Don't speed chilling by placing dough in freezer.)

Roll out dough and line a 9-inch pie pan as directed on page 12. To bake blind, follow directions on page 13, but reduce oven heat to 425°.

Making Sweetened Pastry in a Food Processor

(see Sweetened Short Crusts chart, page 8)

1 Place flour and sugar (and other dry ingredients) in processor bowl. With motor running, drop in butter, one chunk at a time; continue processing until mixture resembles coarse meal.

2 With motor running, drop egg through feed tube. If egg appears to be sticking to sides of processor work bowl, stop motor and run a rubber spatula around bowl, pushing dough into center.

3 Process just until dough begins to hold together—it should still look crumbly. *Do not* process until dough forms a ball, or pastry will be tough. Gather dough into a ball with your hands.

Mixing a Crumb Crust in a Food Processor

(see Crumb Crusts chart, page 9)

1 Break up graham crackers or cookies, dropping pieces into processor work bowl. The smaller the pieces, the more uniform the crumbs will be.

2 Add sugar (and other dry ingredients) to crackers; process, using on-off pulses, until fine crumbs form. Add melted butter; process until butter is evenly distributed.

3 Pour crumb mixture into a 9-inch pie pan and spread to make an even layer. Then press another pie pan into crumb mixture until crust has an even thickness.

Pie Crusts **11**

Rolling, Forming & Baking the Crust

The secret to tender, flaky pastry is in the techniques used to mix and roll the dough. On pages 7 and 8, you'll find directions for making pastry dough; here and on the next page, we tell you how to roll out and shape that perfect crust. Also here are instructions for baking a pastry shell "blind"—without a filling.

ROLLING OUT PASTRY

The directions below tell you how to line a standard pie pan. Essentially the same technique is used to line tart pans, but the edges of a tart crust are often finished a bit differently (see page 41).

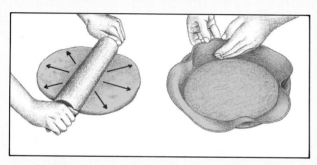

For a single-crust pie. Place chilled dough on a lightly floured board. If you're using a stockinet-covered rolling pin, also dust it lightly with flour. Place rolling pin in center of dough, then roll from center to edge in an even stroke; lift rolling pin as it comes to edge of dough, so edges of pastry won't be thinner than middle. Lift dough and give it a quarter turn after each roll, but avoid excessive handling—that leads to tough, hard crusts. Ideally, the rolled-out pastry circle should be about ⅛ inch thick and 2 inches wider in diameter than pie pan (an 11-inch circle for a 9-inch pan, for example).

To transfer rolled-out dough to pan, roll half the circle loosely around rolling pin, then lift onto ungreased pan. Or fold circle in half and lift onto pan, placing fold across center of pan. Unroll (or unfold) dough and ease it into pan, working out from center with your fingertips to fit dough against pan sides. Don't stretch dough—if you do, crust may shrink down and away from pan sides as it bakes. If dough cracks or tears, just moisten the torn edges and press them back together; or press on a patch made from a moistened scrap of dough.

Next, form a raised edge. Trim dough extending beyond pan rim to ½ inch; then fold overhang

under itself, making dough even with pan rim. Press lightly to seal, bringing part of outer edges of dough down just beneath pan rim and hooking dough onto pan to help hold crust in place during baking.

Finally, make a decorative edge on the crust.

If you're baking the crust blind, follow the directions on page 13; if you want to partially bake it (a good idea for most custard pies), turn to page 29.

For a double-crust pie. For bottom crust, use slightly more than half the dough. Roll out dough and ease into pan as directed at left for a single-crust pie; trim overhang to ½ inch. Spoon filling into shell. Use remaining dough to make a plain or lattice top. Add a top finish, if desired.

To make a plain top, roll out dough to a circle 2 inches wider in diameter than pie pan. Brush edges of bottom crust lightly with water or egg wash (1 egg lightly beaten with 1 tablespoon water). Lift top crust onto pie. Trim, leaving a 1-inch overhang. Then form a raised edge by folding edges of top crust under edges of bottom crust and pinching to seal.

Make a decorative edge and cut a few slashes in the top crust to allow steam to escape during baking. Or cut out decorative vent holes, using a small fancy cookie cutter or an hors d'oeuvre cutter.

LATTICE TOPS

To make either of the lattice tops below, start with ropes of dough (as described for a woven lattice) or flat strips (as described for an easy lattice).

Woven lattice top. Roll dough for top crust between palms to make ten 10-inch ropes. Lightly brush edges of bottom crust with water. Evenly space 5 ropes across filling; carefully fold every other one back onto itself. Then space remaining 5 ropes across pie at right angles to first set, weaving a lattice as shown above. Trim ends of ropes even with edges of bottom crust. Fold edges (and rope ends) under, even with pan rim; press to seal. Then make a decorative edge.

Easy lattice top. Roll dough for top crust to a circle 2 inches wider in diameter than pie pan; cut circle into ¾-inch-wide strips. Lightly brush edges of bottom crust with water. Evenly space half the strips across filling; then evenly space remaining strips across first set, at right angles to them.

Press ends of strips into edges of bottom crust to seal; trim crust even with pan rim. Or trim ends of strips even with edges of bottom crust, then fold edges (and strip ends) under, even with pan rim. Press to seal; make a decorative edge.

DECORATIVE EDGES

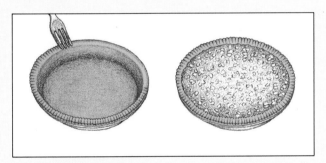

Fork edge. Dip a 4-tined fork into flour. Point tines toward center of pan; firmly press raised edge to pan rim with back of fork tines, making 4 lines. Repeat around edge of pie, positioning fork so each new set of lines partially overlaps the preceding set. (Use the same technique to seal the edges of turnovers.)

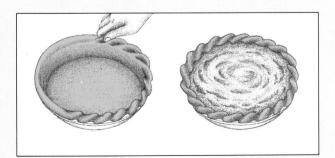

Rope edge. Press thumb on raised edge at an angle to center of pan. With knuckle of index finger, press pastry toward thumb and slightly roll

index finger toward inside of pan. Place thumb in dent left by index finger; press and roll again. Repeat around edge of pie.

Fluted edge. Place tip of index finger on outside of raised edge, pointing to inside of pan. Place thumb and index finger of other hand on inside of raised edge, one on either side of "outside" finger. Pinch pastry up around outside finger. Repeat around edge of pie, making flutes about ½ inch apart. *For a high fluted edge* (for single-crust pies only), pinch pastry up to make higher ridges.

TOP FINISHES

An attractive finish on the top crust makes the difference between an ordinary pie and one that gets rave reviews. For a crust that's sure to be beautifully browned, brush with cream or milk before baking; for a sparkly look, brush crust with cream, then sprinkle lightly with granulated sugar. If you prefer a glossy finish, lightly beat 1 egg with 1 tablespoon water or milk; brush over unbaked crust.

Baked pies also benefit from a finishing touch. Glaze the hot pie with a simple icing made from 2 tablespoons sifted powdered sugar mixed with 1 tablespoon milk; or melt a few tablespoons of currant jelly, then brush over hot crust.

BAKING BLIND (UNFILLED)

Line pie pan with dough as directed on page 12; make a decorative edge. To prevent dough from puffing up unevenly during baking, prick it all over with a fork—but don't prick it all the way through to pan, or juicy fillings will seep through crust. Preheat oven to 450°.

Cut a round of foil to fit inside crust; place in dough shell and gently mold to fit. Fill foil with raw beans or rice or with pie weights (available in cookware stores). Bake for 10 minutes, then lift off foil and beans and continue to bake until lightly browned (4 to 5 more minutes). Place on a rack and let cool completely before filling.

Sweet Pies

It is possible to eat well without lifting a rolling pin. You can easily indulge your sweet tooth without dipping your hands in flour. But if you agree that pies have never gone out of style, you'll enjoy discovering—or rediscovering—the delights of the baker's kitchen.

What better way to bring back fond memories of childhood and home, and to create a happy new tradition for family and friends, than to bake a marvelous pie? Or perhaps you'll choose a tart or cobbler, or a batch of tartlets, turnovers, or dumplings. You'll find many familiar favorites here: warm, spicy apple pie; juicy peach dumplings; chocolate cream pie capped with a mile-high meringue; bubbly rhubarb cobbler.

But if you're looking for new ideas, you'll find those too. Try tiny raspberry barquettes or ricotta rum pie sparked with chocolate bits; or bake a panful of pumpkin pie squares for a new twist on a holiday classic.

Seasonal baking. The rule your grandmother followed when baking fruit pies still makes sense: choose a pie filling that takes advantage of locally grown fruit at the peak of ripeness. You'll be rewarded with the sweetest of fruits and berries—perfect gems to display in an open-faced tart or tartlets or to bake into a pie. (Some fruits have very short seasons, though,

so our recipes often give you the option of using canned or frozen fruits.)

Certain pies seem suited to certain times of year. How can February pass without at least one cherry pie, or the short days of autumn slip by without an excuse to serve chess pie or raisin pie? A freshly baked pie is all the reason you need to celebrate.

How soon to serve? Don't be disappointed if the results of your pie baking don't last. They're not meant to! Most pies taste best within a few hours after baking. Fruit pies are ready to serve as soon as they're cooled enough for the juicy filling to set up a bit— but you can hold them for up to a day at room temperature. Meringue-topped pies should be served soon after they come from the oven; the fluffy topping is especially fragile, and doesn't hold up well for much longer than about 3 hours at room temperature.

What if you really need a pie that can be made well in advance? You still have plenty to choose from: chiffon pies, meringue shell pies, cheesecakes and pies, freezer pies. Freezer pies keep well for up to a month; almost all the others will hold for at least 24 hours.

Choosing a crust. Most of our recipes call for flaky pastry, sweet butter pastry, or a crumb crust. But you may prefer to use your own crust recipe, or to try one of the specialty crusts on page 10. Feel free to substitute, but be sure to choose a crust whose flavor is compatible with the filling and the type of pie.

Year-round enjoyment is yours with Brandied Apricot Tart (recipe on page 44), quickly made with canned apricots.

Fruit Pies

They're all straightforward kitchen masterpieces—pies brimming with pure, fresh fruit flavor, with crusts so tender they melt in the mouth. And there's no better way to showcase each season's fruit than with a delectable pie—open-faced or double-crust, plain or fancy.

But you needn't restrict your fruit pie baking to seasons when fresh fruit is plentiful. Tempting pies can also be made with dried, canned, or frozen fruit—as in Harvest Fruit Pie, for example, or Lattice-top Cherry Pie.

As a rule of thumb, serve fruit pies slightly warm or at room temperature. Pies with dairy products in the filling are an exception to the general rule; refrigerate those and serve them cold.

Fresh Fruit Pie

Fresh, warm-from-the-oven pie with juicy morsels of fruit enveloped in tender, flaky pastry—who can resist such home-baked goodness? At any time of year, you can create delicious pies bursting with sugar and spice and pick-of-the-season fruit. Select one of the fruit fillings from the chart on the facing page; then follow this master recipe for pie assembly. You have a choice of two styles: a traditional double-crust pie or a single-crust pie with a streusel topping.

> **Fruit Filling of your choice (see chart on facing page)**
>
> **Flaky Pastry for a double-crust or single-crust 9-inch pie (page 7)**
>
> 2 **tablespoons butter or margarine (for a double-crust pie only)**
>
> **Streusel Topping (for a single-crust pie only; recipe follows)**

To prepare filling of your choice, mix desired fruit with sugar, cornstarch or tapioca, and suggested flavorings. Determine amount of sugar (within range indicated) by ripeness of fruit and personal taste. (Sugar increases liquid in pie, so if you use the maximum amount of sugar—or if fruit is very juicy—use the maximum amount of cornstarch or tapioca.) Let mixture stand while you roll out pastry.

Place chilled pastry dough on a lightly floured board or pastry cloth. (If you're making a double-crust pie, use slightly more than half the dough.) Roll dough out from center to edges with light, even strokes. Give dough a quarter turn after each stroke; if necessary, lightly sprinkle work surface with flour to prevent sticking. Roll out dough to an 11-inch circle about ⅛ inch thick. Gently fold dough in half. Lift folded dough and place it on a 9-inch pie pan, with fold across center of pan. (Or roll half the circle around rolling pin, then lift onto pan—see photo 5, page 6.) Unfold (or unroll) dough; then, without stretching dough, ease it from center out to rim, using fingertips to fit dough gently up pan sides.

If dough cracks or tears during rolling, simply repair by moistening the torn edges with water, then pressing one edge to the other. Or patch a tear or thin spot by pressing on a moistened scrap of dough (do the same thing if you need to extend dough anywhere around edges of pan).

For a double-crust pie. Trim edges of bottom crust to leave a ½-inch overhang. Fill with fruit mixture and dot with butter. Roll remaining dough to an 11-inch circle; roll half the circle around rolling pin, then place on top of filling and gently unroll to cover filling (or fold dough circle into quarters, place on top of filling, and gently unfold). Trim, leaving a 1-inch overhang; then fold edges of top crust under edges of bottom crust. Make a decorative edge (see page 13). Slash top crust; add a top finish, if desired (see page 13).

For a streusel-topped pie. Trim bottom crust to leave a ½-inch overhang. Fold overhang under, making crust even with pan rim; make a decorative edge (see page 13). Fill with fruit mixture. Prepare Streusel Topping and sprinkle over fruit.

To bake pie. Set oven at temperature indicated on chart. Set pie on a rimmed baking sheet (to catch any drips) and bake on lowest oven rack for recommended time. Check pie after 15 to 20 minutes; if edges are browning too fast, wrap them with a 2 to 3-inch-wide strip of foil. If streusel-topped pie is also browning too fast on top, simply drape entire pie with foil. Bake until filling is bubbly and crust is well browned.

Place pie on a rack and let cool for about 45 minutes before cutting; serve warm. Or let cool to room temperature, then serve. To reheat, bake, uncovered, in a 350° oven until heated through (10 to 15 minutes). Makes 6 to 8 servings.

Streusel Topping. In a bowl, combine 1 cup **all-purpose flour,** ½ cup firmly packed **brown sugar,** and ½ teaspoon **ground cinnamon.** With your fingers, rub in 6 tablespoons firm **butter** or margarine until mixture resembles coarse crumbs. Stir in ½ cup chopped **nuts,** if desired.

FRESH FRUIT PIES

Type of Pie	Fruit	Sugar	Cornstarch or Tapioca*	Flavorings	Baking Temperature	Baking Time
Apple (Granny Smith, Gravenstein, Jonathan, Newtown pippin)—peel, core, and thinly slice						
9″ double crust	8 cups	¾–1 cup	2½–3 tablespoons	1 tsp. ground cinnamon and ¼ tsp. ground ginger	425°	50–60 minutes
9″ streusel top	6 cups	½–¾ cup	1½–2 tablespoons	¾ tsp. ground cinnamon and ¼ tsp. ground ginger	375°	60 minutes
Apricot—remove pits, quarter or slice						
9″ double crust	8 cups	1¼–1½ cups	3½–4 tablespoons	1 tbsp. lemon juice and 1¼ tsp. ground coriander	425°	55–60 minutes
9″ streusel top	6 cups	1–1¼ cups	3–3½ tablespoons	1 tbsp. lemon juice and 1 tsp. ground coriander	425°	75–90 minutes
Berry (blue, black, boysen, logan)						
9″ double crust	6 cups	1½–1¾ cups	3½–4 tablespoons	1 tbsp. lemon juice (blueberry only)	425°	55–60 minutes
9″ streusel top	6 cups	1¼–1½ cups	3½–4 tablespoons	1 tbsp. lemon juice (blueberry only)	425° (blueberry), 375° (others)	75–90 min. (blueberry), 55–60 min. (others)
Cherry, Sweet—remove pits						
9″ double crust	8 cups	1–1¼ cups	2½–3 tablespoons	2 tbsp. lemon juice and ¼ tsp. almond extract (optional)	425° for 15 min., then 350° for 30 min.	45 total minutes
9″ streusel top	6 cups	¾–1 cup	2–2½ tablespoons	1½ tbsp. lemon juice and ¼ tsp. almond extract (optional)	375°	40–45 minutes
Peach or Nectarine—peel (peaches only), pit, and thinly slice						
9″ double crust	8 cups	¾–1 cup	3–3½ tablespoons	2 tbsp. lemon juice and ½ tsp. ground nutmeg	425°	40–50 minutes
9″ streusel top	6 cups	½–¾ cup	2½–3 tablespoons	1½ tbsp. lemon juice and ¼ tsp. ground nutmeg	425°	75 minutes
Plum (Santa Rosa, Nubiana)—pit and slice						
9″ double crust	8 cups	1½–2 cups	6½–7 tablespoons	1 tsp. grated lemon peel and ½ tsp. ground cinnamon	425°	60 minutes
9″ streusel top	6 cups	1–1½ cups	4½–5 tablespoons	¾ tsp. grated lemon peel and ¼ tsp. ground cinnamon	425°	65 minutes

*Use quick-cooking tapioca.

Strawberry Peach Pie

Summertime ... and the cooking should be easy. For warm-weather entertaining, serve a cool chef's salad and crusty bread, then present this beautiful cook-ahead fruit pie.

    Flaky Pastry for a single-crust 9-inch pie (page 7)
4 cups hulled strawberries
¾ cup sugar
¼ cup cornstarch
2 tablespoons lemon juice
    Cheese Filling (recipe follows)
3 cups peeled, sliced peaches
    Sweetened whipped cream (optional)

Preheat oven to 450°. Following directions on pages 12 and 13, roll out pastry, line a 1½-inch-deep 9-inch pie pan, and bake blind. Place on a rack and let cool.

Set aside 5 or 6 strawberries. Crush enough of the remaining berries to make 1½ cups; slice the rest. In a 2 to 3-quart pan, stir together sugar and cornstarch. Add crushed berries and lemon juice. Cook over medium heat, stirring, until mixture boils and thickens. Remove from heat; let stand for 10 minutes. Stir in sliced berries. Let cool.

Prepare Cheese Filling. Spread over bottom and up sides of pastry shell. Top with half the berry mixture; then arrange peach slices (drain well, if juicy) on top. Spoon remaining berry mixture over peaches. Refrigerate for at least 4 hours or for up to 12 hours. Garnish with whipped cream, if desired, and reserved berries. Makes 6 to 8 servings.

Cheese Filling. Beat until smooth: 1 large package (8 oz.) **cream cheese,** softened; 3 tablespoons **sugar;** and 1 tablespoon **orange juice** or milk.

Peach & Sour Cream Pie

(Pictured on facing page)

Ever since the ancient Chinese propagated the first peach, cooks around the world have devised countless ways to highlight the fruit's luscious flavor. Americans like to put peaches in sweet pies like this one—a single-crust beauty filled with sliced peaches in a spiced sour cream custard.

    Nutty Short Pastry for a single-crust 9-inch pie (page 7)
5 cups peeled, sliced peaches
1½ to 2 tablespoons lemon juice
2 eggs
½ cup plus 2 tablespoons sugar
1½ cups sour cream
½ teaspoon *each* grated lemon peel, ground nutmeg, and ground ginger
¼ teaspoon salt
½ recipe Streusel Topping (page 16)

Preheat oven to 400°. Roll out pastry and line a 9-inch pie pan as directed on page 12.

Place peaches in a bowl; sprinkle with lemon juice and stir gently to coat. Set aside. In another bowl, beat eggs, sugar, and sour cream until smooth; mix in lemon peel, nutmeg, ginger, and salt. Pour half the mixture into pastry shell. Arrange peaches on top, then cover with remaining sour cream mixture. Bake for 20 minutes.

Meanwhile, prepare ½ recipe Streusel Topping. Sprinkle over pie; continue to bake until filling is set and crust is well browned (15 to 20 more minutes). Place on a rack and let cool. Makes 6 servings.

Glazed Nectarine Pie

Melted apple jelly makes a quick glaze for sliced nectarines atop a creamy cheese filling.

1 large package (8 oz.) cream cheese, softened
¼ cup sugar
½ teaspoon vanilla
½ cup whipping cream
    Graham Cracker Crust for a 9-inch pie, baked and cooled (page 9)
½ cup plain or mint-flavored apple jelly
3 cups sliced nectarines

In a large bowl of an electric mixer, beat cream cheese, sugar, and vanilla until smooth. With mixer on highest speed, gradually add cream, beating until mixture is the consistency of whipped cream. Spoon into crust; refrigerate for 20 minutes.

In a small pan, heat jelly over low heat, stirring occasionally, until melted; set aside. Arrange nectarines on cream filling, overlapping slices slightly. Evenly spoon jelly over top, completely coating fruit. Refrigerate for at least 1 hour or up to 8 hours. Makes 6 servings.

Peach & Sour Cream Pie

1 Flute edge of pie. Put thumb and index finger on inside of 2 flutes; put other thumb and index finger on outside. Twist to form a "petal" edge.

2 Pour half the sour cream mixture into unbaked crust. Then place lemon-coated peaches in a spiral pattern atop cream, starting at outside edge and working toward center.

3 To retain the spiral fruit pattern, gently pour the remaining sour cream mixture atop peaches, using a small measuring cup or a ladle.

4 Prepare streusel topping while pie bakes; after pie has baked for 20 minutes, evenly crumble streusel over top and return pie to oven.

Apple Custard Pie

Shredded tart apples in a lightly spiced custard fill this unusual version of apple pie.

> Oatmeal Pastry for a single-crust 9-inch pie (page 7)
> 4 eggs
> ¾ cup sugar
> ¼ cup butter or margarine, melted and cooled
> 1 teaspoon vanilla
> ½ teaspoon grated lemon peel
> ¼ teaspoon *each* ground cinnamon and nutmeg
> 3 or 4 large tart apples
> Sweetened whipped cream (optional)

Preheat oven to 425°. Roll out pastry and line a 9-inch pie pan as directed on page 12.

In a large bowl, lightly beat eggs; add sugar and beat until well blended. Stir in butter, vanilla, lemon peel, cinnamon, and nutmeg.

Peel and core apples; then coarsely shred, using a food processor or a shredder with large holes (you should have 3 cups, lightly packed). Stir apples into egg mixture; then spread filling in pastry shell.

Bake on lowest oven rack for 10 minutes. Reduce oven heat to 350° and continue to bake until a knife inserted in center comes out clean (35 to 40 more minutes). Place on a rack and let cool until only slightly warm; then serve. (Or refrigerate pie and serve cold.) Top with whipped cream, if desired. Makes 6 servings.

Lattice-topped Cherry Pie

Mark a day on your February calendar to make this delectable pie. It's sure to dispel the winter doldrums.

> 2 cans (16 oz. *each*) pitted sour cherries
> ⅓ cup *each* granulated sugar and firmly packed brown sugar
> 2½ tablespoons cornstarch
> ¼ teaspoon ground cinnamon
> ⅛ teaspoon almond extract
> Flaky Pastry for a double-crust 9-inch pie (page 7)
> 1 tablespoon butter or margarine

Drain cherries, discarding all but ⅓ cup of the liquid; then place cherries and reserved ⅓ cup liquid in a 2-quart pan. Stir in granulated sugar, brown sugar, cornstarch, and cinnamon. Cook over medium-low heat, stirring, until sugar is dissolved; then simmer for 1 minute. Remove from heat, add almond extract, and let cool.

Preheat oven to 425°. Roll out a little more than half the pastry and line a 9-inch pie pan as directed on page 12. Pour filling into pastry shell; dot with butter. Roll out remaining pastry to an 11-inch circle; cut into ¾-inch-wide strips, then make a woven or easy lattice top (see pages 12 and 13). Bake for 15 minutes; reduce oven heat to 350° and continue to bake until filling is bubbly and crust is browned (35 to 40 more minutes). Place on a rack and let cool before cutting. Makes 6 servings.

Fresh Strawberry Pie

Here's a delicious way to welcome spring: an open-faced pie brimming with glazed fresh strawberries.

> Flaky Pastry for a single-crust 9-inch pie (page 7)
> 1½ cups mashed or puréed strawberries
> ¾ cup water
> 1 tablespoon lemon juice
> ½ cup sugar
> 3 tablespoons cornstarch
> 5 cups halved strawberries
> Sweetened whipped cream

Preheat oven to 450°. Following directions on pages 12 and 13, roll out pastry, line a 1½-inch-deep 9-inch pie pan, and bake blind. Place on a rack and let cool.

Place mashed strawberries, ½ cup of the water, and lemon juice in a 2-quart pan; bring to a boil over medium heat. Strain mixture to remove pulp, then measure liquid. If necessary, simmer to reduce to 1 cup (or add water to make 1 cup).

Return liquid to pan and stir in sugar. Mix cornstarch with remaining ¼ cup water; stir in. Cook over medium heat, stirring, until glaze boils and thickens. Remove from heat; let cool.

Fill pastry shell with 2½ cups of the halved strawberries; pour ⅓ of the glaze over berries. Top with remaining 2½ cups halved berries; pour remaining glaze evenly over top. Refrigerate until glaze is set (about 2 hours) or for up to 8 hours. Serve with whipped cream. Makes 8 servings.

Rhubarb-Strawberry Pie

It's not only seasonal compatibility that makes rhubarb and strawberries a good team; the sweetness of the berries mellows the rhubarb's tart flavor.

> **Flaky Pastry for a double-crust 9-inch pie (page 7)**
> ½ cup *each* granulated sugar and firmly packed brown sugar
> 1 tablespoon cornstarch
> ¼ cup all-purpose flour
> ½ teaspoon ground nutmeg
> 4 cups fresh rhubarb, in ½-inch pieces (about 1⅓ lbs.); or 4 cups frozen rhubarb, thawed and drained
> 2 cups thickly sliced strawberries
> 1 tablespoon orange juice
> 2 tablespoons butter or margarine

Preheat oven to 425°. Roll out a little more than half the pastry and line a 9-inch pie pan as directed on page 12.

In a large bowl, combine granulated sugar, brown sugar, cornstarch, flour, and nutmeg. Add rhubarb, strawberries, and orange juice; mix well. Turn into pastry shell; dot with butter. Roll out remaining pastry to an 11-inch circle and cut into ¾-inch-wide strips; then make a woven or easy lattice top (see pages 12 and 13). Bake until fruit is tender and crust is browned (about 50 minutes). Makes 6 to 8 servings.

Harvest Fruit Pie

Diced dried fruit mix gives this pie its sweet, tangy flavor. If you can't find the packaged mix, just use a combination of raisins and diced dried apricots, peaches, apples, and pears.

> **Flaky Pastry for a single-crust 9-inch pie (page 7)**
> 3 cups (two 6-oz. packages) diced dried mixed fruit
> About 2 cups water
> 2 tablespoons cornstarch
> ½ cup sugar
> 2 teaspoons lemon juice
> 1 cup chopped walnuts
> Vanilla ice cream

Preheat oven to 450°. Following directions on pages 12 and 13, roll out pastry, line a 9-inch pie pan, and bake blind. Place on a rack and let cool.

In a 2-quart pan, combine fruit with 2 cups of the water. Simmer over medium heat, uncovered, stirring frequently, until fruit is soft (5 to 10 minutes). Spoon fruit into a strainer to drain. Measure cooking liquid; if necessary, add water to make 1 cup (or boil to reduce to 1 cup).

In a dry pan, stir together cornstarch and sugar. Add cooking liquid and lemon juice. Cook over medium heat, stirring, until mixture boils and thickens. Stir in drained fruit and walnuts; let cool. Spoon fruit mixture into pastry shell. Cover and refrigerate for at least 4 hours or for up to 24 hours. Serve with ice cream. Makes 6 to 8 servings.

Ricotta Berry Pie

Berry filling bubbles beneath a ricotta topping.

> **Flaky Pastry for a single-crust 9-inch pie (page 7)**
> 2½ cups blackberries or boysenberries
> ¾ cup sugar
> 1½ tablespoons quick-cooking tapioca
> ¾ teaspoon ground cinnamon
> 8 ounces ricotta cheese
> 1 egg (at room temperature), separated
> ¼ teaspoon salt
> ½ cup half-and-half (light cream)
> ¾ teaspoon grated lemon peel
> 1 tablespoon lemon juice

Preheat oven to 425°. Roll out pastry and line a 9-inch pie pan as directed on page 12.

In a bowl, stir together berries, ½ cup of the sugar, tapioca, and ½ teaspoon of the cinnamon; let stand for 5 minutes. In a food processor or blender, whirl ricotta cheese, egg yolk, salt, half-and-half, the remaining ¼ cup sugar, lemon peel, and lemon juice until smooth. In large bowl of an electric mixer, beat egg white until it holds soft peaks; gently fold in cheese mixture.

Turn berry mixture into pastry shell; evenly spread cheese mixture on top. Sprinkle with remaining ¼ teaspoon cinnamon. Bake for 10 minutes; then reduce oven heat to 350° and continue to bake until topping appears firm when pan is gently shaken (about 30 more minutes). Place on a rack and let cool to room temperature; serve, or refrigerate for up to 24 hours. Makes 6 servings.

Deep-dish Blueberry Pie

1 With sharp knife, cut through pastry dough, using inverted dish as guide. Measuring from outline just made, cut a ring the width of dish rim.

2 Place blueberry mixture in dish. Cut through dough ring at ends. Fit one ring half onto dish rim; fit on other half, overlapping ends slightly. Trim off excess dough. Brush rim with egg.

3 Dot blueberry mixture with butter. Carefully place top crust on dish, making edges of dough rim and top crust as even as possible. Press gently to seal.

4 Press down firmly on dough rim with back of fork tines; repeat around edge of pie. Decorate top with pastry cutouts.

Deep-dish Blueberry Pie

(Pictured on facing page and on front cover)

Deep-dish pies are simple to make: just pour the filling into a 1-quart dish, cover with flaky pastry, and bake. Choose a ceramic or pottery container, and make sure the rim is at least ½ inch wide; a narrower rim won't provide enough support for the top crust, which may collapse into the filling. To allow steam to escape during baking, make a few slashes in the crust—or cut out fancy shapes with a small cookie cutter.

This type of pie is a little juicier than the traditional double-crust pie, so serve it in bowls. Topped with cream or a scoop of ice cream, it's a wonderful old-fashioned dessert treat.

- 4 **cups blueberries or huckleberries**
- ¾ **cup sugar**
- 3 **tablespoons all-purpose flour**
- ¾ **teaspoon ground cinnamon**
- ¼ **teaspoon ground nutmeg**
- ⅛ **teaspoon salt**
- 1 **tablespoon lemon juice**
  Flaky Pastry for a single-crust 9-inch pie (page 7)
- 1 **egg lightly beaten with 1 tablespoon water**
- 1 **to 2 tablespoons butter or margarine**

Preheat oven to 450°. Rinse and drain blueberries; place in a large bowl. Add sugar, flour, cinnamon, nutmeg, salt, and lemon juice; stir just until dry ingredients are moistened. Cover blueberry mixture and set aside.

On a lightly floured board, roll out pastry to about 2 inches wider and longer than a 1-quart rimmed baking dish. Measure width of dish rim; then gently invert dish onto dough. Rest blade of a sharp knife against dish; cut around edge of dish. Measuring out from the outline just made, cut a ring of dough the width of dish rim. Remove excess dough; lift off dish.

Spoon blueberry mixture into dish. Cut vents in top crust; cut through outer ring of dough at both ends. Carefully fit each half of dough ring onto rim, overlapping ends slightly; cut off excess. Brush egg mixture over dough ring.

Dot filling with butter. Lift top crust onto dish, lining up edges of crust and dough rim; press gently together.

Dip a 4-tined fork into egg mixture; then firmly press dough rim and top crust together with fork tines, positioning fork so each new set of lines par-tially overlaps the preceding set. Brush top with egg mixture. If you used a cookie cutter to make vents, brush backs of pastry cutouts with egg mixture; place cutouts on crust and brush again with egg mixture.

Place a baking sheet on lowest oven rack to catch drips. Bake pie for 10 minutes; then reduce oven heat to 350° and bake until pastry is browned (about 30 more minutes). Place pie on a rack and let cool for 15 minutes; spoon into individual bowls. Makes 4 to 6 servings.

Deep-dish Apple Pie

Follow directions for **Deep-dish Blueberry Pie,** but substitute 5 cups peeled, sliced **Golden Delicious apples** for blueberries. Decrease sugar to ½ cup and cinnamon to ½ teaspoon; increase lemon juice to 2 tablespoons.

Deep-dish Peach Pie

Follow directions for **Deep-dish Blueberry Pie,** but substitute 4 cups peeled, sliced **peaches** for blueberries. Substitute 2 tablespoons **cornstarch** for flour. Omit cinnamon and add ½ teaspoon grated **lemon peel.**

Deep-dish Blackberry Pie

Follow directions for **Deep-dish Blueberry Pie,** but substitute 4 cups **fresh or unsweetened frozen blackberries** for blueberries. (Before using frozen berries, thaw to room temperature and place in a strainer to drain; discard liquid.) Substitute 2 tablespoons **cornstarch** for flour; omit cinnamon and nutmeg and add ½ teaspoon grated **lemon peel.**

Deep-dish Cherry Pie

Follow directions for **Deep-dish Blueberry Pie,** but substitute 4 cups pitted **fresh or unsweetened frozen cherries** for blueberries. (Before using frozen cherries, thaw to room temperature and place in a strainer to drain; discard liquid.) Substitute 3 tablespoons **cornstarch** for flour; omit cinnamon and nutmeg and add 1 teaspoon grated **lemon peel** and ¼ teaspoon **almond extract.**

Deep-dish Plum Pie

Follow directions for **Deep-dish Blueberry Pie,** but substitute 4 cups pitted, sliced **Santa Rosa or Nubiana plums** for blueberries. Substitute 2½ tablespoons **cornstarch** for flour; reduce cinnamon to ½ teaspoon. Omit nutmeg and lemon juice and add 1 teaspoon grated **lemon peel.**

Old-fashioned Mince Pie

You can't buy mincemeat as good as the one in this pie. It's the old-fashioned kind, full of beef, brandy, fruit, and sweet, pungent spices.

> **Flaky Pastry for a double-crust 9-inch pie (page 7)**
> 1 **quart Old-fashioned Mincemeat (at right)**
> 1 **cup chopped walnuts**
> 2 **tablespoons brandy**
> **Whipped Hard Sauce (page 33)**

Preheat oven to 425°. Roll out a little more than half the pastry and line a 9-inch pie pan as directed on page 12. Combine mincemeat, walnuts, and brandy; spoon into pastry shell. Roll out remaining pastry and place on pie; seal and flute edges (see page 13) and slash top. Bake in lower third of oven until crust is golden brown (35 to 40 minutes).

Place pie on a rack and let cool for about 1 hour; serve warm with hard sauce. Makes 6 to 8 servings.

No-bake Blueberry Pie

Pure blueberry flavor with no distractions. That's the best way to describe this quick-to-fix pie filling.

> **Flaky Pastry for a single-crust 9-inch pie (page 7)**
> 4 **cups blueberries**
> ¾ **cup sugar**
> 2½ **tablespoons cornstarch**
> 2 **tablespoons** *each* **water and lemon juice**
> ½ **teaspoon ground cinnamon**
> **Sweetened whipped cream**

Preheat oven to 450°. Following directions on pages 12 and 13, roll out pastry, line a 9-inch pie pan, and bake blind; place on a rack and let cool.

Fill pastry shell with 3 cups of the blueberries. In a pan, crush remaining 1 cup berries and stir in sugar; cook over medium heat, stirring, until sugar is dissolved. Stir together cornstarch, water, and lemon juice; add to berry mixture along with cinnamon. Cook, stirring, until mixture boils and thickens; spoon over berries in pastry shell. Refrigerate for at least 1 hour or for up to 8 hours. Serve with whipped cream. Makes 6 servings.

Old-fashioned Mincemeat

If you plan to use this mincemeat in pies, freeze it in 1-quart containers. Pack in smaller quantities for use in turnovers and tarts.

> 1 **pound lean beef stew meat, cut into 1-inch cubes**
> ½ **pound beef suet**
> 2 **pounds tart green apples (unpeeled), cored and quartered**
> ¼ **pound citron**
> 1 **orange (unpeeled), seeded**
> 1 **lemon (unpeeled), seeded**
> 1½ **cups** *each* **granulated sugar and firmly packed brown sugar**
> 1 **package (15 oz.) dark (seedless) raisins**
> 1 **package (15 oz.) golden raisins**
> 1 **package (10 oz.) currants**
> ½ **cup dark molasses**
> 2 **cups** *each* **cider vinegar and apple juice**
> 1 **teaspoon** *each* **ground nutmeg, cloves, cinnamon, mace, and allspice**
> 1½ **teaspoons salt**
> 2 **cups brandy (or 2 cups apple juice and ½ teaspoon brandy flavoring)**

Place beef in a 5-quart pan and add just enough water to cover. Bring to a boil over high heat; then reduce heat, cover, and simmer until meat is tender (about 1½ hours). Lift out meat and set aside. Measure cooking liquid; if necessary, boil to reduce to 1 cup (or add water to make 1 cup). Set aside.

Using a food processor or a food chopper fitted with a coarse blade, chop or grind meat, suet, apples, citron, orange, and lemon. Place in a 6 to 8-quart pan; add cooking liquid, granulated sugar, brown sugar, raisins, currants, molasses, vinegar, apple juice, spices, and salt. Simmer over medium heat, uncovered, until thick but still juicy (about 1¼ hours); stir often as mincemeat thickens. Stir in brandy; simmer, stirring often, until thickened again (about 30 more minutes). Remove from heat and let cool.

Spoon into freezer containers, allowing 1 inch head space. Cover and refrigerate for up to 1 week or freeze for up to 6 months. Makes 4 quarts.

Pear Pepper Pie

Choose full-flavored winter pears, such as Bosc, Anjou, or Comice, to make this delectable pie. The filling is lightly seasoned with white pepper and enriched with whipping cream.

> **Cream Cheese Pastry for a double-crust 9-inch pie (page 10)**
> ¾ **cup sugar**
> ¼ **cup quick-cooking tapioca**
> ¼ **teaspoon white pepper**
> 8 **cups peeled, thinly sliced firm-ripe pears, such as Bosc, Anjou, or Comice**
> 1 **egg, lightly beaten**
> ¼ **cup whipping cream**

Preheat oven to 400°. Roll out a little more than half the pastry and line a 9-inch pie pan as directed on page 12.

In a large bowl, stir together sugar, tapioca, and pepper. Gently stir pears into sugar mixture; turn into pastry shell. Roll out remaining pastry and place on pie; seal and flute edges (see page 13), then slash top and brush with egg. Bake until filling is bubbly (about 1 hour).

Cut a 3-inch hole in center of top crust and lift out pastry; slowly pour in cream, lifting pears slightly with a knife so cream seeps in. Replace cutout pastry, place pie on a rack, and let cool until lukewarm. Makes 6 to 8 servings.

Cranberry Crunch Pie

You spread cream cheese in a pastry shell, then add a sweet-tart cranberry-apple filling and a spicy walnut streusel. The result? A festive pie with a wonderful contrast of smooth and crunchy textures.

> **Flaky Pastry for a single-crust 9-inch pie (page 7)**
> 1 **large package (8 oz.) cream cheese, softened**
> ⅓ **cup firmly packed brown sugar**
> 2 **tablespoons cornstarch**
> ⅛ **teaspoon salt**
> 1 **can (16 oz.) whole cranberry sauce**
> 2 **cups peeled, chopped tart apples**
> **Walnut Streusel (recipe follows)**

Preheat oven to 450°. Following directions on pages 12 and 13, roll out pastry, line a 1½-inch-deep 9-inch pie pan, and bake blind. Place on a rack and let cool.

In small bowl of an electric mixer, beat cream cheese until smooth; spread on bottom of pastry shell. In a bowl, combine sugar, cornstarch, and salt. Stir in cranberry sauce and apples. Spoon mixture evenly over cream cheese. Prepare streusel; sprinkle over cranberry mixture.

Bake in a 375° oven until streusel is golden brown (about 45 minutes). Check pie after 15 to 20 minutes; if crust or streusel is overbrowning, drape pie loosely with foil. Place on a rack and let cool; then refrigerate until cold. Makes 6 to 8 servings.

Walnut Streusel. In a bowl, combine ⅓ cup **all-purpose flour,** ½ cup chopped **walnuts,** 3 tablespoons firmly packed **brown sugar,** and ¼ teaspoon **ground cinnamon.** With your fingers, rub in ¼ cup firm **butter** or margarine until mixture resembles coarse crumbs.

Concord Grape Pie

To seed tight-skinned grapes, you must cut each grape in half, then pick out the seeds by hand. But the job is much easier with Concords—they're slip-skinned. You just squeeze the pulp from the skins and strain out the seeds to make this beautiful, rich-tasting purple pie.

> 5 **cups rinsed, stemmed Concord grapes (about 2 lbs.)**
> 1 **cup sugar**
> ⅛ **teaspoon *each* salt and ground cloves**
> 3½ **tablespoons quick-cooking tapioca**
> **Flaky Pastry for a double-crust 9-inch pie (page 7)**

Squeeze each grape and slip out pulp into a small pan; reserve grape skins. Cook pulp over low heat until hot and soft, stirring and mashing with a fork. Press through a strainer, then let cool. Combine cooled pulp with reserved skins, sugar, salt, cloves, and tapioca. Set aside.

Preheat oven to 425°. Roll out a little more than half the pastry and line a 9-inch pie pan as directed on page 12. Spoon in filling. Roll out remaining pastry and place on pie; seal and flute edges (see page 13) and slash top. Bake until well browned (35 to 40 minutes). Place on a rack and let cool to room temperature. Makes 6 to 8 servings.

Fruit Dumplings

Fruit dumplings are simple and homey—nothing more than sweetened fruit wrapped in biscuit dough or pastry. They're every bit as good for a leisurely weekend breakfast as for dessert.

Peach Dumplings

Because they bake in syrup, these dumplings are soft on the bottom, flaky on top.

    Baking Syrup (recipe follows)
 ⅓ cup sugar
 1 teaspoon ground cinnamon
 ¼ teaspoon ground nutmeg
 2 tablespoons finely chopped almonds
 3 peaches or nectarines
    Lemon juice
    Flaky Pastry for a double-crust 9-inch pie (page 7)
 1 tablespoon butter or margarine
    Cream or sweetened whipped cream

Prepare Baking Syrup and set aside. In a bowl, combine sugar, cinnamon, nutmeg, and almonds; set aside. Peel, halve, and pit peaches (or halve and pit nectarines—do not peel); coat with lemon juice. Set aside.

Preheat oven to 425°. On a lightly floured board, roll out pastry to a 12 by 18-inch rectangle; cut into six 6-inch squares. Center a peach half, pitted side up, on each square. Sprinkle ⅙ of the sugar mixture in hollow of each peach half, then dot peaches evenly with butter. Brush edges of pastry lightly with water; fold and seal pastry around peaches as shown in photos 2, 3, and 4 on the facing page.

Arrange dumplings slightly apart in a 9 by 13-inch baking pan; pour syrup around them. Bake until fruit is tender and pastry is golden brown (35 to 40 minutes). Let cool for at least 30 minutes. Ladle a spoonful of the syrup over each dumpling; top with cream. Makes 6.

Baking Syrup. In a 2-quart pan, bring 2 cups **water,** 1 cup **sugar,** ½ teaspoon **ground cinnamon,** and 3 tablespoons **butter** or margarine to a boil over high heat. Reduce heat; simmer, uncovered, for 3 minutes. Remove from heat.

Apple Chutney Dumplings

(Pictured on facing page)

A piquant chutney filling makes these apple dumplings extra special.

 2 tablespoons *each* raisins, chopped Major Grey's chutney, and chopped pecans
 3 tablespoons firmly packed brown sugar
 3 small Golden Delicious apples
    Lemon juice
 2 cups all-purpose flour
 2 teaspoons baking powder
 ½ teaspoon salt
 ½ cup solid vegetable shortening
 3 tablespoons butter or margarine, melted
 ⅓ cup milk
 1 egg beaten with 1 tablespoon water
 6 pecan halves
    Ginger Syrup (recipe follows)

Stir together raisins, chutney, chopped pecans, and sugar; set aside. Peel and core apples; cut in half, coat with lemon juice, and set aside.

In a bowl, combine flour, baking powder, and salt. With a pastry blender or 2 knives, cut in shortening until coarse crumbs form. Add butter and milk all at once; stir just until dough holds together. Gather into a ball.

Preheat oven to 375°. On a floured board, roll out dough to a 12 by 18-inch rectangle. Cut into six 6-inch squares. Center an apple half, cored side up, on each square; mound ⅙ of the chutney filling in hollow of each apple.

Brush a border of egg mixture around edges of each square; then fold and seal dough around apple as shown in photos 2, 3, and 4 on the facing page. Dip bottoms of pecan halves in egg; press one half on each dumpling. Place dumplings slightly apart in a buttered 9 by 13-inch baking pan. Bake for 30 minutes, then brush with some of the egg mixture; don't let it drip onto pan or dumplings will stick. Continue to bake until dumplings are lightly browned (10 to 15 more minutes).

Prepare Ginger Syrup. Pour over warm dumplings. Pass remaining syrup at the table. Makes 6.

Ginger Syrup. In a 1 to 2-quart pan, combine 1½ cups firmly packed **brown sugar,** ¾ cup **water,** 3 tablespoons **butter** or margarine, 1 tablespoon **lemon juice,** and ½ teaspoon **ground ginger.** Boil over high heat until thickened (about 5 minutes).

Apple Chutney Dumplings

Center an apple half on each dough square; fill cavity with chutney mixture. Brush a ½-inch-wide border of egg mixture all round edges of square.

2 Bring 2 opposite corners of dough square up over apple half, overlapping tips slightly. Press gently to seal.

3 Fold other 2 corners to center, overlapping slightly; press into center to seal.

4 Pinch all 4 seams together firmly. Make sure there aren't any holes in dough, or filling will ooze out and dough will split apart as it bakes.

Cobblers

Fresh fruit cobblers offer homey, old-fashioned appeal... a treasure of warm, spiced fruit topped with rich biscuit dough.

Peach Cobbler

Fresh fruit bakes to succulent perfection beneath cutouts of biscuit dough. Choose peaches, nectarines, or rhubarb for the filling; make the cutouts in any shape that suits your fancy.

    6 cups peeled, sliced peaches or sliced
       nectarines (or some of each)
       About 1 cup sugar
    3 tablespoons cornstarch
    ¾ teaspoon ground nutmeg
    ¾ teaspoon vanilla
    1½ tablespoons lemon juice
    1½ tablespoons butter or margarine
       Biscuit Dough (recipe follows)
       Milk

Preheat oven to 450°. Place peaches in a large bowl. In a small bowl, combine 1 cup of the sugar, cornstarch, and nutmeg. Add to peaches with vanilla and lemon juice; mix thoroughly. Spoon peach mixture into a shallow 1½-quart baking dish; dot with butter. Set aside.

Prepare Biscuit Dough and pat to a thickness of ½ inch on a lightly floured board. Using a 2½ to 3-inch cookie cutter, cut out shapes and place about 1 inch apart on top of fruit. Carefully push scraps together and cut out more shapes, if needed, to cover top of cobbler. Brush dough with milk; sprinkle with sugar.

Bake for 10 minutes. Reduce oven heat to 400° and continue to bake until fruit is bubbly and biscuits are browned on top (about 25 more minutes). Place on a rack and let cool for at least 15 minutes; serve warm. Makes 6 to 8 servings.

Biscuit Dough. In a bowl, sift together 1 cup **all-purpose flour,** 1 teaspoon **baking powder,** and ¼ teaspoon **salt.** Using a pastry blender or 2 knives, cut in 2½ tablespoons *each* **solid vegetable shortening** and firm **butter** until mixture resembles coarse meal. Pour in ⅓ cup **cold water** and stir with a fork until dough cleans sides of bowl.

Rhubarb Cobbler

Follow directions for **Peach Cobbler,** but substitute 2 pounds **rhubarb,** cut into ¾-inch lengths (about 6 cups), for peaches. Increase sugar in filling to 1½ cups. Omit nutmeg, vanilla, and lemon juice; add 1 teaspoon **grated lemon peel.**

Berry Roly-Poly

A roly-poly is simply a cobbler that's shaped into pinwheels of dough and fruit, then baked in a sweet syrup. As with all cobblers, this combination of fruit and biscuit dough tastes best when topped with vanilla or nut-flavored ice cream.

    1¾ cups hot water
    1 cup plus 6 tablespoons sugar
    2 cups all-purpose flour
    1 tablespoon baking powder
    1 teaspoon salt
    6 tablespoons solid vegetable shortening
    ⅔ cup milk
    ¼ cup butter or margarine, melted
    5 cups fresh boysenberries or blackberries
       (or unsweetened frozen berries, thawed
       and drained)
    ¼ teaspoon ground cinnamon
       Vanilla or nut-flavored ice cream

Preheat oven to 450°. In a small pan, combine hot water and 1 cup of the sugar; simmer over low heat for 5 minutes, then pour into a greased 9 by 13-inch baking dish. Let cool.

In a large bowl, combine flour, 2 tablespoons of the sugar, baking powder, and salt. Using a pastry blender or 2 knives, cut in shortening until mixture resembles coarse meal. Stir in milk and butter.

Gather dough into a ball and knead 10 times on a floured board. Roll out to an 8 by 12-inch rectangle. Distribute 2 cups of the berries evenly across dough; sprinkle with cinnamon and remaining 4 tablespoons sugar. Starting with a short end, roll up dough; pinch seam securely to seal.

Cut roll into eight 1-inch-thick slices; arrange, cut side up, in syrup in baking dish. Surround slices with remaining 3 cups berries, pushing berries down into syrup.

Bake until biscuit dough is richly browned (about 25 minutes). Place on a rack and let cool slightly; serve warm, topping each portion with ice cream. Makes 8 servings.

Custard Pies

Custard pies are a good study in contrasts. When made primarily with eggs, milk or cream, and sugar, the filling is soft, tender, and delicately flavored. Add a puréed vegetable to the egg-milk base, as in pumpkin or squash pie, and the filling takes on a quiet body that's nicely balanced with spices. Replace the milk in the base with large amounts of sugar, honey, or corn syrup, and the custard becomes a translucent binding to surround chunky nuts, plump raisins, and more.

When you make custard pies, it's important to avoid overcooking. Overbaking makes a milk-based filling tough and watery, while a sugar-based filling becomes granular. Don't worry if the filling still looks soft in the center when you take the pie from the oven; it will set up as it cools.

Old-fashioned Custard Pie

Our custard pie is extra rich and creamy, since it's made almost entirely with half-and-half.

Flaky Pastry for a single-crust 9-inch pie (page 7)
- 4 eggs
- ½ cup sugar
- ¼ teaspoon salt
- ½ cup milk
- 1 teaspoon vanilla
- 2 cups half-and-half (light cream)
- ¼ teaspoon ground nutmeg

Preheat oven to 425°. Roll out pastry and line a 1½-inch-deep 9-inch pie pan as directed on page 12, making a high fluted edge. Partially bake as directed at right.

Lightly beat eggs with a wire whisk; whisk in sugar, salt, milk, and vanilla. Heat half-and-half just to scalding; slowly whisk into egg mixture. Pour into pastry shell; sprinkle with nutmeg.

Bake in lower third of oven for 15 minutes. Reduce oven heat to 350° and continue to bake until a knife inserted slightly off center comes out clean (about 25 more minutes). Place on a rack and let cool to room temperature; serve, or refrigerate for up to 24 hours. Makes 6 to 8 servings.

Chess Pie

A glass of port and a sliver of pie before a crackling fire—what better way to entertain friends on a nippy autumn evening?

Flaky Pastry for a single-crust 9-inch pie (page 7)
- 3 eggs
- 1 cup sugar
- ¼ teaspoon salt
- ½ cup (¼ lb.) butter or margarine, melted and cooled
- 1 teaspoon vanilla
- 1 cup *each* raisins and coarsely chopped walnuts

Preheat oven to 350°. Roll out pastry and line a 9-inch pie pan as directed on page 12.

In a large bowl, beat eggs, sugar, salt, butter, and vanilla until well blended. Stir in raisins and walnuts. Pour filling into pastry shell.

Bake on lowest rack of oven until filling jiggles only slightly in center when pan is gently shaken (about 40 minutes). Place on a rack and let cool to room temperature; serve, or refrigerate for up to 24 hours. Makes 6 to 8 servings.

How to Partially Bake a Pie Crust

Though pie fillings typically bake in an unbaked shell, it's best to partially bake the pastry before adding most milk-based custard fillings. If these are poured into an unbaked crust, you may end up with soggy pastry.

Preheat oven to 425°. Roll out pastry and line pie pan as directed on page 13 for baking blind, but *do not prick crust*. Cut a circle of foil to fit in pie shell; then line shell with foil, molding it up sides. Half-fill with raw beans or rice or with pie weights. Bake for 10 minutes. Lift off foil and beans; bake for 5 more minutes. Place on a rack and let cool.

If crust begins to overbrown when you bake shell the final time (with filling added), cover pie loosely with foil.

Creamy Pumpkin Pie Squares

1 Using a pastry blender or 2 knives, cut butter into flour mixture until particles are the size of small peas.

2 Sprinkle crumbly dough over pan bottom. Using fingertips, press dough evenly over bottom and sides of pan to within ¼ inch of rim. Bake until lightly browned.

3 Pour pumpkin mixture over crust, taking care not to pour any of it between baked crust and pan—if you do, pieces will be difficult to remove after baking.

4 Bake until filling jiggles only slightly in center when pan is gently shaken. Gently spread sour cream mixture over hot pumpkin custard.

Creamy Pumpkin Pie Squares

(Pictured on facing page)

Here's the perfect choice when it's your turn to bake pies for a large-family holiday meal. The crust can be made a day ahead; you can add the filling and bake the pie hours before serving.

    1½ cups all-purpose flour
    ¾   cup quick-cooking rolled oats
    1½ cups firmly packed brown sugar
    ¾   cup (¼ lb. plus ¼ cup) butter or margarine,
         cut into chunks
    3   eggs
    1   can (16 oz.) pumpkin
    1   can (13 oz.) evaporated milk
    1   teaspoon *each* ground cinnamon and vanilla
    ½   teaspoon *each* ground ginger, ground
         nutmeg, and salt
    ¼   teaspoon ground cloves
        Sour Cream Topping (recipe follows)
    1   cup chopped walnuts or almonds

In a large bowl, stir together flour, oats, and ¾ cup of the sugar. Using a pastry blender or 2 knives, cut in butter until particles are about the size of small peas. Firmly press mixture over bottom and up sides of a 10 by 15-inch rimmed baking pan. (At this point, you may cover crust with foil and let stand at room temperature until next day.)

Preheat oven to 350°. Bake crust on lowest rack of oven until lightly browned (about 20 minutes). Meanwhile, in a bowl, lightly beat eggs. Add pumpkin, milk, cinnamon, vanilla, ginger, nutmeg, salt, cloves, and remaining ¾ cup sugar; stir until smooth.

Remove crust from oven and pour filling over it; spread filling evenly with a spatula. Return to oven and continue to bake until filling jiggles only slightly in center when pan is gently shaken (about 20 more minutes). Meanwhile, prepare Sour Cream Topping.

Remove pie from oven and spread with topping. Return to oven and bake for 10 more minutes. Remove from oven; sprinkle with walnuts. Place on a rack and let cool to room temperature; serve, or cover loosely with foil and let stand for up to 6 hours. Cut into rectangles. Makes about 15 servings.

Sour Cream Topping. In a bowl, stir together 1½ cups **sour cream,** 6 tablespoons **sugar,** and 2 teaspoons **vanilla** until smooth.

Old-fashioned Pumpkin Pie

The sweet, spicy molasses flavor of this pie comes through best at room temperature, so if the pie has been refrigerated, remove it from the refrigerator 30 minutes before serving.

        **Flaky Pastry for a single-crust 10-inch pie
        (page 7)**
    1   can (16 oz.) pumpkin or 2 cups mashed
         cooked winter squash (about 2 lbs. acorn,
         banana, butternut, or Hubbard)
    1¼ cups half-and-half (light cream) or
         evaporated milk
    2   eggs
    ⅓   cup sour cream
    ¾   cup firmly packed brown sugar
    ¼   cup light molasses
    1   tablespoon all-purpose flour
    1   teaspoon ground cinnamon
    ½   teaspoon *each* ground nutmeg, ground
         ginger, salt, and vanilla
    ¼   teaspoon ground cloves
    1   cup whipping cream
    ¼   cup chopped candied ginger

Preheat oven to 425°. Roll out pastry and line a 10-inch pie pan as directed on page 12, making a high fluted edge. Partially bake as directed on page 29.

In a large bowl, beat pumpkin, half-and-half, eggs, sour cream, sugar, molasses, flour, cinnamon, nutmeg, ground ginger, salt, vanilla, and cloves until smoothly blended. Pour into pastry shell.

Bake in lower third of oven for 15 minutes. Reduce oven heat to 350° and continue to bake until a knife inserted slightly off center comes out clean (40 to 45 more minutes). Place on a rack and let cool to room temperature; serve, or refrigerate for up to 24 hours. Remove from refrigerator 30 minutes before serving.

Whip cream until it holds soft peaks; fold in candied ginger. Top each slice of pie with a dollop of cream. Makes 8 to 10 servings.

Sweet Yam Pie

Follow directions for **Old-fashioned Pumpkin Pie,** but substitute 2 cups mashed **cooked yams** or sweet potatoes for pumpkin. Increase sugar to 1 cup; omit molasses. Omit candied ginger; garnish pie with **sweetened whipped cream** and sprinkle with chopped **cashews** or sliced almonds.

Buttermilk Pie

Buttermilk pie is very American—there isn't anything else quite like it! The custard is tangy, buttery, and refreshing.

Flaky Pastry for a single-crust 9-inch pie (page 7)
- 1 cup sugar
- 2 tablespoons all-purpose flour
- 1 cup buttermilk
- 3 eggs, lightly beaten
- ⅓ cup butter or margarine, melted and cooled
- ½ teaspoon grated lemon peel
- 1½ tablespoons fresh lemon juice
- ¼ teaspoon ground nutmeg

Preheat oven to 425°. Roll out pastry and line a 1½-inch-deep 9-inch pie pan as directed on page 12. Partially bake as directed on page 29.

In a large bowl, stir together sugar and flour with a wire whisk; then whisk in buttermilk, eggs, butter, lemon peel, and lemon juice, blending until smooth. Pour into pastry shell and sprinkle with nutmeg.

Bake in lower third of oven for 15 minutes. Reduce oven heat to 350° and continue to bake until filling jiggles only slightly in center when pan is gently shaken (about 25 more minutes). Place on a rack and let cool to room temperature; cut into wedges and serve, or refrigerate for up to 24 hours. Makes 6 to 8 servings.

Lemon Cake Pie

As this pie bakes, a cakelike topping forms over the custardy, sweet-tart lemon filling.

Flaky Pastry for a single-crust 9-inch pie (page 7)
- 1½ cups sugar
- 2 tablespoons butter or margarine, melted and cooled
- ⅓ cup all-purpose flour
- ¼ teaspoon salt
- ½ teaspoon grated lemon peel
- 5 tablespoons fresh lemon juice
- 3 eggs (at room temperature), separated
- 1¼ cups milk

Preheat oven to 375°. Roll out pastry and line a 9-inch pie pan as directed on page 12.

In a large bowl, stir together sugar and butter; blend in flour, salt, lemon peel, and lemon juice. In another bowl, beat egg yolks; then beat in milk. Add milk mixture to lemon mixture and stir well.

In a clean, dry bowl, beat egg whites until they hold moist, stiff peaks; gently fold into lemon-milk mixture. Pour filling into pastry shell.

Bake on lowest rack of oven until top is richly browned and feels set when lightly touched (45 to 55 minutes). Place on a rack and let cool to room temperature; serve, or refrigerate for up to 6 hours. Makes 6 to 8 servings.

Spicy Raisin Pie

Plump, sweet raisins in a tangy buttermilk custard nestle inside this spicy two-crust pie.

Flaky Pastry for a double-crust 9-inch pie (page 7)
- ¾ cup sugar
- 2 tablespoons all-purpose flour
- ½ teaspoon *each* ground cinnamon and nutmeg
- ¼ teaspoon *each* ground allspice and salt
- 1 egg
- 1 cup buttermilk
- 1 tablespoon cider vinegar
- 2 cups raisins
- Milk
- Vanilla ice cream or sweetened whipped cream (optional)

Preheat oven to 425°. Roll out a little more than half the pastry and line a 1½-inch-deep 9-inch pie pan as directed on page 12.

In a large bowl, combine sugar, flour, cinnamon, nutmeg, allspice, and salt. In another bowl, lightly beat egg; stir in buttermilk and vinegar. Add to sugar mixture; stir well. Stir in raisins. Pour into pastry shell; stir gently to distribute raisins.

Roll out remaining pastry and place on pie; seal and flute edges (see page 13), and slash top. Brush top lightly with milk. Bake in lower third of oven for 15 minutes. Reduce oven heat to 350° and continue to bake until crust is golden brown (about 30 more minutes). Place on rack and let cool for 30 minutes before cutting. Serve with ice cream or whipped cream, if desired. When pie has cooled completely, refrigerate for up to 24 hours. Makes 6 to 8 servings.

Peanut Coconut Raisin Pie

This pie contains the goodies you find in trail mix—peanuts, coconut, and raisins—bound together in a brown sugar custard.

  Flaky Pastry for a single-crust 9-inch pie (page 7)
 2 **eggs**
 ¾ **cup firmly packed brown sugar**
 ½ **cup (¼ lb.) butter or margarine, melted and cooled**
 1 **teaspoon vanilla**
 1 **cup chopped salted peanuts**
 ½ **cup raisins**
 ½ **cup sweetened flaked coconut**

Preheat oven to 350°. Roll out pastry and line a 9-inch pie pan as directed on page 12. In a bowl, beat eggs, sugar, butter, and vanilla until well blended. Then add peanuts, raisins, and coconut and stir until combined. Pour filling into pastry shell.

Bake until top of pie is golden brown and filling jiggles only slightly in center when pan is gently shaken (35 to 40 minutes). Place on a rack and let cool to room temperature; serve, or refrigerate for up to 24 hours. Makes 6 to 8 servings.

Pecan Pie

Southern cooks bake pecan pie in dozens of tasty variations—some lighter, some darker, even a few with chocolate. This lightly spiced, caramel-like version has chopped pecans in the middle, pecan halves on top.

  Flaky Pastry for a single-crust 9-inch pie (page 7)
 2 **eggs (at room temperature), separated**
 ½ **cup firmly packed brown sugar**
 ⅛ **teaspoon salt**
 ½ **teaspoon ground cinnamon**
 1 **tablespoon all-purpose flour**
 ¼ **cup butter or margarine, melted and cooled**
 ½ **teaspoon vanilla**
 1 **cup dark corn syrup**
 ¾ **cup coarsely chopped pecans**
 ½ **cup pecan halves**

Preheat oven to 350°. Roll out pastry and line a 9-inch pie pan as directed on page 12.

In a large bowl, lightly beat egg yolks. Add sugar, salt, cinnamon, flour, butter, vanilla, and corn syrup and beat until well blended.

In another bowl, beat egg whites until they hold moist, stiff peaks; gently fold into yolk mixture. Fold in chopped pecans. Pour filling into pastry shell and arrange pecan halves on top.

Bake on lowest rack of oven until a knife inserted slightly off center comes out clean—45 to 50 minutes. (If pecans on top begin to turn too brown, cover pie loosely with foil.) Place on a rack and let cool to room temperature; serve, or refrigerate for up to 24 hours. Makes 6 to 8 servings.

Crunchy Walnut Pie

Try this lightly spiced walnut pie for dessert after a holiday dinner. We suggest topping each slice with a rich brandy-flavored hard sauce, but you can serve the pie plain if you prefer.

  Flaky Pastry for a single-crust 9-inch pie (page 7)
 3 **eggs**
 ½ **cup firmly packed brown sugar**
 1 **cup light corn syrup**
 ¼ **teaspoon salt**
 1 **teaspoon *each* ground cinnamon and vanilla**
 ¼ **cup butter or margarine, melted and cooled**
 1 **cup broken walnuts or walnut halves**
  Whipped Hard Sauce (optional; recipe follows)

Preheat oven to 375°. Roll out pastry and line a 1½-inch-deep 9-inch pie pan as directed on page 12.

In a bowl, beat eggs, sugar, corn syrup, salt, cinnamon, vanilla, and butter until well blended; then stir in walnuts. Pour filling into pastry shell.

Bake on lowest rack of oven until filling jiggles only slightly in center when pan is gently shaken (about 50 minutes). Place on a rack and let cool until slightly warm. Meanwhile, prepare hard sauce, if desired; top each slice of pie with a dollop of sauce. Makes 6 to 8 servings.

Whipped Hard Sauce. In a bowl, blend together ¼ cup **butter,** softened; 1 cup **powdered sugar;** and 1 tablespoon **brandy.** Whip ¼ cup **whipping cream** until it holds soft peaks; fold into creamed mixture. Cover and refrigerate for up to 12 hours.

Cream Pies

Exquisitely simple, a cream pie is nothing more than a pudding in a pie shell. The term "cream" describes the smooth texture of the filling; it doesn't refer to use of cream as an ingredient.

Cream pie fillings are cooked on top of the range, then poured into a baked pie shell. You can use a crumb crust if you prefer, but a flaky pastry shell is our first choice—it's strong enough to support the soft filling without crumbling apart when the pie is cut and served.

Cornstarch and flour are the traditional thickeners for cream pie fillings. Flour makes an opaque, relatively sturdy filling; cornstarch-thickened fillings are softer, with a shinier, more translucent look. We prefer to use a cornstarch-flour combination, which makes a filling with the best qualities of both starches. The cornstarch-flour pairing also helps keep the filling smooth as it cooks.

Vanilla Cream Pie

World-famous pies—stop here! Many a highway restaurant has built its reputation on vanilla cream pie or one of its variations, and so can you. These are family-pleasing pies, simple, sweet, and very satisfying.

> **Flaky Pastry for a single-crust 9-inch pie (page 7)**
> 4 **egg yolks**
> ¼ **cup all-purpose flour**
> 2 **tablespoons cornstarch**
> ¾ **cup sugar**
> ¼ **teaspoon salt**
> 3 **cups milk**
> 3 **tablespoons butter or margarine**
> 1½ **teaspoons vanilla**
> **Meringue Topping (recipe follows) or sweetened whipped cream**

Preheat oven to 450°. Following directions on pages 12 and 13, roll out pastry, line a 1½-inch-deep 9-inch pie pan, and bake blind. Place on a rack and let cool. If you plan to use Meringue Topping, reduce oven heat to 375°.

In a bowl, beat egg yolks; set aside. In a heavy 3-quart pan, stir together flour, cornstarch, sugar, and salt with a wire whisk. Gradually whisk in milk, blending until smooth. Cook over medium heat, stirring constantly, until mixture thickens and comes to a full boil. Boil, stirring constantly, for 1 minute.

Stir about ½ cup of the hot filling into egg yolks; then pour yolk mixture into pan. Cook, stirring, for 2 minutes. Remove from heat; add butter and vanilla. Stir until butter is melted, then pour filling into pastry shell.

Immediately prepare Meringue Topping (if desired); spread over pie and bake as directed below. Place pie on a rack and let cool to room temperature. Serve within 3 hours (topping begins to break down if pie is held longer).

If you plan to serve pie with whipped cream, cover hot filling with plastic wrap after pouring it into pastry shell. Place on a rack and let cool to room temperature; serve, or refrigerate for up to 24 hours. To serve, remove plastic wrap and cover pie with whipped cream. Makes 6 to 8 servings.

Meringue Topping. Preheat oven to 375°. In large bowl of an electric mixer, beat 4 **egg whites** (at room temperature) and ¼ teaspoon **cream of tartar** until frothy. Add 8 tablespoons **sugar**, 1 tablespoon at a time, beating well after each addition; continue to beat until sugar is dissolved and meringue holds glossy, stiff peaks. Thoroughly blend in ½ teaspoon **vanilla.**

Spoon meringue onto warm pie filling; then spread in an even layer with a spatula, making sure meringue touches all edges of pastry. (This anchors meringue to crust and prevents it from shrinking during baking.) Make swirls in meringue with spatula. Bake until meringue is lightly browned (5 to 7 minutes).

Chocolate Cream Pie
(Pictured on facing page)

Follow directions for **Vanilla Cream Pie,** but reduce cornstarch in filling to 1 tablespoon and increase sugar to 1 cup. Break up (or chop) 3 ounces **unsweetened chocolate** and add to pan after stirring in milk. Reduce butter to 2 tablespoons. Top with **Meringue Topping;** or let pie cool, then top with **sweetened whipped cream.**

Banana Cream Pie

Prepare filling as directed for **Vanilla Cream Pie.** Slice 2 large **bananas;** spread half the slices in bottom of pastry shell, then pour in half the filling. Repeat with remaining bananas and filling. Top with **Meringue Topping;** or let pie cool, then top with **sweetened whipped cream.**

(Continued on page 36)

Chocolate Cream Pie

To prevent egg yolks from curdling, stir about ½ cup of the hot milk mixture into lightly beaten yolks; then pour yolk mixture back into pan.

2 Yolks help thicken filling, giving it a pudding-like consistency. *As soon as* filling has thickened, pour it into pastry shell. Don't overcook filling—it will become runny.

3 Carefully spread meringue over warm filling, spreading it out to crust all around pie. Sealing meringue to crust helps prevent it from shrinking away from edges of pie during baking.

4 If not using meringue, cover hot filling with plastic wrap to prevent a skin from forming. Let cool; remove plastic and top pie with whipped cream.

Coconut Cream Pie

Follow directions for **Vanilla Cream Pie** (page 34), but stir 1 cup **sweetened flaked coconut** into thickened filling. Let pie cool, then top with **sweetened whipped cream,** and sprinkle with ½ cup **sweetened flaked coconut, toasted.**

Lemon Meringue Pie

This refreshingly tart pie is a perfect conclusion for a springtime meal. (Be sure to use *fresh* lemon juice in the filling.)

    Flaky Pastry for a single-crust 9-inch pie (page 7)
- 3 **egg yolks**
- 2 **tablespoons all-purpose flour**
- 5 **tablespoons cornstarch**
- 1¼ **cups sugar**
- ¼ **teaspoon salt**
- 2 **cups water**
- 2 **tablespoons butter or margarine**
- 1½ **teaspoons grated lemon peel**
- ½ **cup fresh lemon juice**
    Meringue Topping (page 34)

Preheat oven to 450°. Following directions on pages 12 and 13, roll out pastry and line a 1½-inch-deep 9-inch pie pan, making a high fluted edge; then bake blind. Place on a rack and let cool. Reduce oven heat to 375°.

In a bowl, beat egg yolks; set aside. In a heavy 3-quart pan, stir together flour, cornstarch, sugar, and salt with a wire whisk. Gradually whisk in water, blending until smooth. Add butter. Cook over medium heat, stirring, until mixture thickens and comes to a full boil. Boil, stirring constantly, for 1 minute.

Stir about ½ cup of the hot filling into egg yolks; then pour yolk mixture into remaining filling in pan and stir to blend well. Cook, stirring constantly, for 2 minutes. Remove from heat. Stir in lemon peel and lemon juice, then pour into pastry shell.

Immediately prepare Meringue Topping, using 3 egg whites and 6 tablespoons sugar; spread over pie and bake as directed on page 34. Place pie on a rack and let cool to room temperature. Pie tastes best if served within 3 hours after cooling; topping begins to break down if pie is held longer. Makes 6 to 8 servings.

Butterscotch Pie

Butterscotch lovers take note: this pie offers a double temptation. Caramelized white sugar and brown sugar team up to give the filling a rich, old-fashioned flavor.

    Flaky Pastry for a single-crust 10-inch pie (page 7)
- 3 **egg yolks**
- 2 **tablespoons all-purpose flour**
- ¼ **cup cornstarch**
- ⅔ **cup firmly packed brown sugar**
- ¼ **teaspoon salt**
- 3 **cups milk**
- ½ **cup granulated sugar**
- 3 **tablespoons butter or margarine**
- ¼ **cup water**
- 1 **teaspoon vanilla**
    Sweetened whipped cream
    Sliced almonds

Preheat oven to 450°. Following directions on pages 12 and 13, roll out pastry, line a 10-inch pie pan, and bake blind. Place on a rack and let cool.

In a bowl, beat egg yolks; set aside. In a heavy 3-quart pan, stir together flour, cornstarch, brown sugar, and salt with a wire whisk. Gradually whisk in 1½ cups of the milk, blending until smooth. Set aside.

In another heavy 3-quart pan, combine granulated sugar, butter, and water. Cook over medium heat, stirring constantly, until sugar caramelizes and turns light golden (10 to 12 minutes). Slowly and carefully, pour in remaining 1½ cups milk. (Milk will spatter slightly as it hits caramelized sugar.) Continue to cook, stirring, until caramel is dissolved.

Pour caramel mixture into cornstarch-milk mixture. Cook over medium heat, stirring, until mixture thickens and comes to a full boil. Boil, stirring, for 1 minute.

Stir about ½ cup of the hot filling into egg yolks; then pour mixture into pan. Cook, stirring constantly, for 2 minutes. Remove pan from heat and add vanilla; stir to blend well. Pour filling into pastry shell.

Cover filling with plastic wrap. Place pie on a rack and let cool to room temperature; serve, or refrigerate for up to 24 hours. At serving time, remove plastic wrap and cut pie into individual servings. Top each slice with a spoonful of sweetened whipped cream and a sprinkling of almonds. Makes 8 to 10 servings.

Chiffon Pies

A chiffon pie filling is an airy combination of beaten egg whites or whipped cream (or both) and a flavored base, held in billowy suspension with gelatin. Because the filling takes time to set, these are ideal pies for times when you want to get a head start on cooking.

To ensure success with chiffon pies, you must first soften the gelatin granules in a cold liquid, then dissolve them completely with heat and stirring. (When you no longer see any granules on the stirring spoon, the gelatin is fully dissolved.)

Once the gelatin is dissolved, you need to thicken the mixture before folding in beaten egg whites or whipped cream. Refrigerate it for 30 to 45 minutes, stirring occasionally as gelatin thickens to prevent lumps; or stir over ice water for 10 to 20 minutes. If mixture becomes so firm that you can't fold in whipped ingredients, set pan over hot water and whisk until mixture is smooth; then re-chill.

Cranberry Persimmon Pie

You need fully ripened persimmons to make this tart-sweet pie; if they're at all unripe, they'll have an astringent flavor. If the fruit feels hard, let it stand at room temperature for a few days—until it's very soft, with a jellylike texture.

    1   envelope unflavored gelatin
    ¼   cup cold water
    2   or 3 very ripe medium-size persimmons
    1   can (16 oz.) whole cranberry sauce
    1   teaspoon grated orange peel
    2   egg whites (at room temperature)
    2   tablespoons sugar
    1   cup whipping cream
        Nutty Graham Crust for a 9-inch pie, baked and cooled (page 9)

In a 1-quart pan, sprinkle gelatin over cold water; let soften for several minutes. Then stir over low heat until gelatin is dissolved.

Scoop out persimmon flesh; discard skin, seeds, and stems. Whirl flesh in a blender or food processor until smooth; you should have 1 cup purée. Add dissolved gelatin, cranberry sauce, and orange peel; whirl until very smooth. Refrigerate

(or stir over ice water) until mixture mounds slightly when dropped from a spoon.

In large bowl of an electric mixer, beat egg whites until frothy. Add sugar, 1 tablespoon at a time, beating well after each addition. Continue to beat until sugar is dissolved and meringue holds glossy, stiff peaks. In another bowl, whip ½ cup of the cream until it holds soft peaks. Fold gelatin mixture into meringue, then fold in whipped cream. Turn into crust. Refrigerate until firm (3 to 4 hours) or for up to 24 hours.

Whip remaining ½ cup cream until it holds soft peaks; spoon over pie. Makes 6 to 8 servings.

Grasshopper Pie

Feeling nostalgic? Put on a tape of big band music, turn down the lights, and serve this very special pie. It's as appealing today at it was years ago, when it was created to duplicate the flavor of a popular drink called a "grasshopper."

    1½ teaspoons unflavored gelatin (about ½ envelope)
    1⅓ cups whipping cream
    4   egg yolks
    ¼   cup sugar
    ¼   cup *each* white crème de cacao and green crème de menthe
        Chocolate Crumb Crust for a 9-inch pie, baked and cooled (page 9)
        Semisweet chocolate curls (page 40)

In a small pan, sprinkle gelatin over ⅓ cup of the cream; let soften for several minutes, then stir over low heat until gelatin is dissolved. Remove from heat and set aside.

In large bowl of an electric mixer, beat egg yolks until light and lemon colored. Gradually add sugar, beating until mixture falls from beaters in a thick ribbon. Beat in crème de cacao and crème de menthe. Stir in gelatin mixture. Refrigerate (or stir over ice water) until custard mounds slightly when dropped from a spoon.

In another bowl, whip remaining 1 cup cream until it holds soft peaks; then fold whipped cream into crème de menthe mixture. Turn into crust and refrigerate until firm (about 4 hours) or for up to 24 hours. (Or, for a frostier pie, freeze solid. To store for more than 1 day, wrap frozen pie airtight as directed on page 50.) Garnish with chocolate curls. Makes 8 servings.

Chocolate-topped Rum Pie

1 Sprinkle powdered gelatin over water, then let stand to soften. Gelatin will swell and absorb all the water; it will dissolve when stirred into hot custard.

2 To prevent meringue from collapsing as you fold in custard, push part of meringue away from side of bowl; slowly pour custard into space and fold custard and meringue together.

3 Rum chiffon filling will be as thick as whipped cream. Pour into baked pastry shell and refrigerate until set.

4 Melt butter and chocolate; add sugar and egg yolk, beating until smooth. Pour over filling; smooth out with a small spatula, completely covering pie.

Chocolate-topped Rum Pie

(Pictured on facing page)

Here's a black-bottom pie in reverse. Instead of hiding under the rum-flavored filling, the chocolate layer is right on top. (Chocolate lovers may want to use our Chocolate-Nut Crust, page 10, in place of a flaky pastry shell.)

    Flaky Pastry for a single-crust 9-inch pie (page 7)
1 envelope unflavored gelatin
¼ cup cold water
5 egg yolks
¼ teaspoon salt
1 cup granulated sugar
½ cup hot water
⅓ cup light or dark rum
4 egg whites (at room temperature)
6 tablespoons butter, softened
1½ ounces unsweetened chocolate
6 tablespoons powdered sugar

Preheat oven to 450°. Following directions on pages 12 and 13, roll out pastry, line a 9-inch pie pan, and bake blind. Place on a rack and let cool.

In a bowl, sprinkle gelatin over cold water; let soften for several minutes. In a heavy 2-quart pan, beat 4 of the egg yolks well with a wire whisk. Whisk in salt and ½ cup of the granulated sugar. Gradually stir in hot water. Cook over medium-low heat, stirring constantly, until custard has thickened enough to lightly coat a metal spoon. Remove from heat; add softened gelatin and stir until dissolved. Let cool slightly, then stir in rum. Refrigerate (or stir over ice water) until custard mounds slightly when dropped from a spoon.

In large bowl of an electric mixer, beat egg whites until frothy. Add remaining ½ cup granulated sugar, 1 tablespoon at a time, beating well after each addition. Continue to beat until sugar is dissolved and meringue holds glossy, stiff peaks. Fold custard into meringue; turn into pastry shell and refrigerate until firm (3 to 4 hours).

In the top of a double boiler over simmering water, melt butter and chocolate, stirring until smooth. Remove from heat; add powdered sugar and stir until smooth. Lightly beat remaining 1 egg yolk, then blend into chocolate mixture. Immediately pour mixture over filling and smooth out with a small spatula. Refrigerate until firm (about 30 minutes) or for up to 24 hours. Makes 6 to 8 servings.

Coconut Chiffon Pie

This pie tastes like coconut eggnog. The airy vanilla custard filling is piled into a crisp coconut crust, then topped with more coconut.

¾ cup sweetened flaked or shredded coconut
1 teaspoon ground cinnamon
¼ teaspoon ground nutmeg
1 envelope unflavored gelatin
¼ cup cold milk
4 eggs (at room temperature), separated
⅛ teaspoon salt
½ cup sugar
1 cup hot milk
1 teaspoon vanilla
½ cup whipping cream
    Macaroon Crumb Crust for a 9-inch pie, baked and cooled (page 9)

Preheat oven to 350°. In a shallow baking pan, stir together coconut, cinnamon, and nutmeg; spread out evenly. Toast until coconut is golden brown (about 8 minutes), stirring frequently so coconut toasts evenly. Let cool.

In a bowl, sprinkle gelatin over cold milk; let soften for several minutes. In a heavy 2-quart pan, beat egg yolks well with a wire whisk. Whisk in salt and 6 tablespoons of the sugar. Gradually stir in hot milk. Cook over medium-low heat, stirring, until custard has thickened enough to lightly coat a metal spoon. Remove from heat; add softened gelatin and stir until dissolved. Stir in vanilla. Refrigerate (or stir over ice water) until custard mounds slightly when dropped from a spoon.

In a large bowl of an electric mixer, beat egg whites until frothy. Add remaining 2 tablespoons sugar, 1 tablespoon at a time, beating well after each addition. Continue to beat until sugar is dissolved and meringue holds glossy, stiff peaks. In another bowl, whip cream until it holds soft peaks. Fold custard into meringue, then fold in whipped cream.

Spoon half the filling into crust; top with half the coconut. Repeat with remaining filling and coconut. Refrigerate until firm (about 4 hours) or for up to 24 hours. Makes 6 to 8 servings.

Double Coconut Pie

Follow directions for **Coconut Chiffon Pie,** but substitute 1 cup hot **half-and-half** (light cream) for the 1 cup hot milk and ½ teaspoon **coconut extract** for the vanilla.

Irish Coffee Pie

What a delicious way to conclude a meal—serve your guests whiskey-laced coffee-and-cream, in the form of a luscious pie. If you wish to serve coffee as a beverage, too, demitasse is the perfect choice.

    1 **envelope unflavored gelatin**
   ¼ **cup cold milk**
    2 **eggs (at room temperature), separated**
   ¾ **cup sugar**
    2 **tablespoons instant coffee powder**
   ¾ **cup hot milk**
    2 **tablespoons Irish whiskey or ¼ teaspoon brandy flavoring**
    1 **cup whipping cream**
      Chocolate-Nut Crust for a 9-inch pie, baked and cooled (page 10)
      Milk chocolate curls (at right)

In a bowl, sprinkle gelatin over cold milk; let soften for several minutes. In a heavy 2-quart pan, beat egg yolks well with a wire whisk. Whisk in ½ cup of the sugar.

Dissolve coffee powder in hot milk, then gradually stir milk mixture into yolk mixture. Cook over medium-low heat, stirring constantly, until custard has thickened enough to lightly coat a metal spoon. Remove from heat; add softened gelatin and stir until dissolved. Let cool slightly, then stir in whiskey. Refrigerate (or stir over ice water) until custard mounds slightly when dropped from a spoon.

In large bowl of an electric mixer, beat egg whites until frothy. Add remaining ¼ cup sugar, 1 tablespoon at a time, beating well after each addition. Continue to beat until sugar is dissolved and meringue holds glossy, stiff peaks. In another bowl, whip cream until it holds soft peaks. Fold custard into meringue, then fold in whipped cream. Turn into crust. Refrigerate until firm (3 to 4 hours) or for up to 24 hours. Garnish with chocolate curls. Makes 6 to 8 servings.

Orange Chiffon Pie

Prescription for a spring tonic: crisp, flaky pastry; tangy orange filling; smooth whipped cream; and crunchy toasted almonds. Even Grandma would approve!

      Flaky Pastry for a single-crust 9-inch pie (page 7)
    1 **envelope unflavored gelatin**
   ¼ **cup cold water**
    3 **eggs (at room temperature), separated**
   ⅛ **teaspoon salt**
   ¾ **cup sugar**
   ¾ **cup hot water**
    1 **can (6 oz.) frozen orange juice concentrate**
    3 **tablespoons fresh lemon juice**
    1 **cup whipping cream**
   ¼ **cup slivered almonds, toasted**

Preheat oven to 450°. Following directions on pages 12 and 13, roll out pastry, line a 9-inch pie pan, and bake blind. Place on a rack and let cool.

In a bowl, sprinkle gelatin over cold water; let soften for several minutes. In a heavy 2-quart pan, beat egg yolks well with a wire whisk. Whisk in salt and ½ cup of the sugar. Gradually stir in hot water. Cook over medium-low heat, stirring, until custard has thickened enough to lightly coat a metal spoon. Remove from heat; add softened gelatin and stir until dissolved. Add orange juice concentrate and lemon juice; stir until concentrate is melted. Refrigerate (or stir over ice water) until custard mounds slightly when dropped from a spoon.

In large bowl of an electric mixer, beat egg whites until frothy. Add remaining ¼ cup sugar, 1 tablespoon at a time, beating well after each addition. Continue to beat until sugar is dissolved and meringue holds glossy, stiff peaks.

In another bowl, whip ½ cup of the cream until it holds soft peaks. Fold custard into meringue, then fold in whipped cream. Turn into pastry shell. Refrigerate until firm (3 to 4 hours) or for up to 24 hours. Whip remaining ½ cup cream; garnish pie with cream and almonds. Makes 6 to 8 servings.

Making Chocolate Curls

Chocolate curls made from semisweet or milk chocolate make a professional-looking garnish for many pies. Work with a thick piece of chocolate, and make sure it's at room temperature (cold chocolate is too hard to "shave" easily). Draw the blade of a vegetable peeler firmly across surface of chocolate to make thick, curly shapes (see photo 4, page 75). To prevent the curls from melting, lift them onto the pie with a spatula; don't pick them up with your fingers.

Tarts

Though pies and tarts have a strong family resemblance, they also differ in certain ways. Tarts are shallower than pies, and they're usually open-faced —not covered with a crust, streusel, or meringue, or even topped with swirls of whipped cream. The pastry differs, too. Pies call for a flaky pastry so tender it needs the support of a pie pan; tart crusts are more crisp than flaky, and sturdy enough to stand on their own when removed from the baking pan. And unlike pie dough, tart pastry tolerates handling and re-rolling without becoming tough.

The classic tart pan is a shallow metal pan made in two parts: a removable bottom and a fluted ring that forms the sides. To remove a baked tart from its pan, you just push up on the bottom; since the baked crust shrinks away from the pan sides, the tart lifts out easily. You can also form tart shells in a fluted ceramic quiche dish or a standard pie pan, then serve the tart right from its pan.

Miniature tarts—often called "tartlets"—hold only a small amount of filling, so they don't require as sturdy a crust as a full-size tart. You can use flaky pastry if you prefer.

Metal tartlet pans come in a variety of sizes and shapes; tartlet shells can also be molded over the bottoms of muffin cups (pleat pastry around cups, alternating cups so pastry shells don't touch each other). Tartlets that bake with a filling can be formed in muffin cups or custard cups.

How to line a tart pan. You can press tart pastry into the pan if you wish, but rolling is faster and produces a crust with a more even thickness. Roll out pastry to a circle about ⅛ inch thick and 2 inches wider in diameter than tart pan. Transfer pastry to pan (see photo 1, page 43); gently ease over bottom and sides of pan. Then roll rolling pin across top of pan, cutting dough off even with pan rim.

Pear & Almond Tart

This elegant tart looks as lovely as it tastes. Poached pear halves top a layer of almond cream; the lemony crust and tangy apricot glaze nicely complement the flavors of fruit and filling.

If peaches are in season, you might want to try our fresh peach variation. Arrange the peach slices in concentric rings on top of the almond filling.

Lemon Pastry for an 11-inch tart (page 8)
Poached Pears (recipe follows) or 1 can (about 29 oz.) pear halves
½ recipe Uncooked Pastry Cream (page 71)
¼ teaspoon almond extract
2 tablespoons kirsch (optional)
⅔ cup apricot jam
¼ cup sliced almonds

Preheat oven to 350°. Roll out pastry and line an 11-inch fluted tart pan with a removable bottom as directed at left. Prick pastry all over with a fork; bake in lower third of oven until golden brown (22 to 25 minutes). Place on a rack and let cool.

While pastry shell cools, prepare Poached Pears. (Or drain canned pear halves well; reserve syrup for other uses, if desired.)

Prepare Uncooked Pastry Cream; stir in almond extract and, if desired, kirsch. Spread pastry cream evenly in pastry shell. Decoratively arrange pear halves atop filling, with stem ends pointing toward center of tart and cut sides down. Gently push pear halves into filling. Cover tart and refrigerate until filling is firm (about 1 hour).

Place jam in a small pan and stir over low heat just until melted. Press through a strainer to remove bits of fruit; then let cool for 5 minutes. Lightly brush or drizzle glaze over pear halves and filling. Refrigerate tart until glaze is set (about 15 minutes) or for up to 4 hours.

While tart chills, spread almonds in a shallow baking pan and toast in a 350° oven until golden (about 8 minutes); stir almonds often so they toast evenly. Let cool.

Just before serving, remove pan sides and garnish tart with almonds. Makes 10 to 12 servings.

Poached Pears. In a 4 to 5-quart pan, combine 1½ cups **water,** ¾ cup **sugar,** and 1 teaspoon *each* grated **lemon peel** and **vanilla.** Bring to a boil over high heat; then boil, stirring constantly, until sugar is dissolved.

Peel 4 medium-size **pears;** cut in half lengthwise, then cut out cores. Sprinkle all over with **lemon juice.** Place pear halves, cut side down, in syrup; reduce heat, cover, and simmer until pears are tender when pierced (about 10 minutes). Lift from syrup and drain well.

Fresh Peach Tart

Follow directions for **Pear & Almond Tart,** but substitute 3 cups peeled, sliced **peaches** for pears. Drizzle peaches with 2 teaspoons **lemon juice;** do not poach. Drain peaches before arranging atop tart. Garnish tart with toasted sliced almonds or with **mint sprigs.**

Wine-poached Fig Tart

Impressive tarts don't always have to be made with fresh fruit. Here's one that features dried figs plumped in spiced wine.

    About 1½ cups dry red wine
 ½ cup sugar
 1 cinnamon stick (2 to 3 inches long)
    Yellow part of peel from 1 lemon
 1 tablespoon lemon juice
 ½ teaspoon freshly ground black pepper
 1 pound moist-pack dried figs (about 2 cups lightly packed)
    Toasted Almond Cream (recipe follows)
    Sweet Butter Pastry made with 2 cups flour (page 8)
 2 tablespoons red currant jelly

In a 3-quart pan, combine 1½ cups of the wine, sugar, cinnamon stick, lemon peel, lemon juice, and pepper. Bring to a boil over high heat; boil, stirring, until sugar is dissolved. Add figs; reduce heat, cover, and simmer until figs are plump and soft (20 to 30 minutes). Remove from heat and let cool in syrup to room temperature.

Drain figs, reserving syrup. Trim off woody stem ends, then set figs aside. Prepare Toasted Almond Cream and set aside.

Preheat oven to 400°. Press pastry evenly over bottom and 1 inch up sides of a 10 or 11-inch spring-form pan. Spread almond cream in pastry shell, then arrange figs over cream. Bake in lower third of oven until filling swells up around fruit and is richly browned (about 45 minutes). Place tart on a rack and let stand for at least 45 minutes before removing pan sides and cutting.

Meanwhile, measure reserved fig syrup; if necessary, boil to reduce to ⅔ cup or add wine to make ⅔ cup. Combine syrup and jelly in a small pan; stir over low heat until jelly is melted. Serve syrup hot or at room temperature to spoon over wedges of tart. Makes 10 to 12 servings.

Toasted Almond Cream. In a food processor or blender, whirl ¾ cup **blanched almonds** until powdery. Pour into a wide frying pan; stir over medium heat until nuts turn slightly darker and smell toasted (3 to 4 minutes); take care not to scorch.

Remove from heat and stir in ¾ cup **powdered sugar** and 2 tablespoons **all-purpose flour;** let cool. Using an electric mixer, blend nut mixture thoroughly with ½ cup (¼ lb.) **butter** or margarine, softened. Then add 1 **egg,** 1 **egg yolk,** and 2 teaspoons **vanilla;** blend well.

Fresh Fruit & Custard Tart

(Pictured on facing page)

Just by varying the fresh fruit topping, you can use this recipe to make dozens of different tarts. You start with a crisp pastry shell and a creamy filling— then arrange a mosaic of whole or sliced fruit atop, in whatever pattern suits your fancy. Mix and match colors and flavors—choose from blackberries, blueberries, loganberries, strawberries, raspberries, orange slices, figs, kiwis, and plums. You can also use peaches, apricots, nectarines, apples, bananas, and pears—but to prevent these fruits from darkening, sprinkle the slices with lemon juice immediately after cutting. Drain fruit well before arranging it atop the tart.

    Sweet Butter Pastry for an 11-inch tart (page 8)
    French Pastry Cream (recipe follows)
    Fresh fruit (suggestions above)

Preheat oven to 350°. Roll out pastry and line an 11-inch fluted tart pan with a removable bottom as directed on page 41. Prick pastry all over with a fork, then line pastry shell with foil and partially fill with raw beans or rice. Bake for 15 minutes, then lift off foil and beans. (Beans can be used as pie weights several more times.) Continue to bake shell until lightly browned (7 to 10 more minutes). Place on a rack and let cool.

Meanwhile, prepare and refrigerate French Pastry Cream. Fill pastry shell with slightly set pastry cream; refrigerate for at least 1 hour. Decorate top of tart with fresh fruit of your choice. Serve immediately; or refrigerate, uncovered, for 1 to 3 hours. Remove pan sides before serving. Makes 10 to 12 servings.

French Pastry Cream. In a 2-quart pan, combine 1 cup **sugar,** ½ cup **cornstarch,** ¼ teaspoon **salt,** and 1 cup **milk.** Stir until cornstarch is dissolved. In another pan, scald 2 cups **milk** over medium heat; add slowly to sugar mixture, stirring constantly. Bring to a boil over medium heat, stirring; boil and stir constantly for 2 minutes, then remove from heat.

Beat 4 **egg yolks** until thick and lemon colored. Stir half the milk mixture into yolks, then stir all back into pan. Cook over low heat, stirring, until mixture is thick enough to mound slightly when dropped from a spoon (5 to 7 minutes). Pour into a bowl; stir in 1 teaspoon **vanilla.** Cover pastry cream with a piece of plastic wrap, pushing plastic directly onto surface of cream. Refrigerate until slightly set (about 45 minutes).

Fresh Fruit & Custard Tart

Loosely wrap rolled-out dough around rolling pin and transfer to tart pan. Gently unroll over pan; carefully fit pastry into pan.

2 Press rolling pin down firmly on pan rim; roll it across pan top. Sharp edge of pan will trim pastry even with pan rim. Prick all over with a fork to prevent crust from puffing up.

3 Line shell with foil; partially fill with raw beans or rice. Bake for 15 minutes; lift off foil and beans. Continue to bake shell until lightly browned (7 to 10 more minutes).

4 Beat custard constantly to keep it smooth. Finished custard should fall in thick ribbon; it will thicken as it cools.

Nut Mosaic Tart

This golden, honey-sweetened tart is reminiscent of pecan pie, though not as sweet. The filling is made with unsalted nuts; if you can find only salted macadamias or pistachios, wrap them in a towel and rub briskly to remove as much salt as possible before using in this recipe.

      3 cups unsalted nuts—whole hazelnuts
         (filberts), macadamias, blanched almonds,
         or pistachios; or walnut or pecan halves;
         or a combination
         Sweet Butter Pastry for an 11-inch tart
         (page 8)
      3 eggs
      1 cup honey
      ½ teaspoon grated orange peel
      1 teaspoon vanilla
      ¼ cup butter or margarine, melted and cooled
         Sweetened whipped cream (optional)

Preheat oven to 350°. Spread nuts in a shallow baking pan and bake until lightly toasted (about 10 minutes); let cool.

Roll out pastry and line an 11-inch fluted tart pan with a removable bottom as directed on page 41.

In a bowl, beat eggs, honey, orange peel, vanilla, and butter until well blended. Stir in nuts. Pour into pastry shell; bake in lower third of oven until top is golden brown (about 40 minutes). Place on a rack and let cool; then remove pan sides. Cut tart into wedges; top each serving with a spoonful of sweetened whipped cream, if desired. Makes 10 to 12 servings.

Brandied Apricot Tart

(Pictured on page 14)

Because this quick tart uses canned rather than fresh apricots, you can enjoy it any time of year.

         Sweet Butter Pastry for a 10-inch tart (page 8)
      ¾ cup apricot jam
      2 tablespoons apricot brandy or apricot-
         flavored liqueur
      4 cans (17 oz. *each*) peeled whole apricots,
         drained well, cut in half, and pitted
      2 tablespoons slivered almonds, toasted

Preheat oven to 350°. Roll out pastry and line a 10-inch fluted tart pan with a removable bottom as directed on page 41. Prick pastry all over with a fork. Bake in lower third of oven for 8 minutes; place on a rack and let cool.

Meanwhile, in a small pan, combine jam and brandy; stir over low heat until jam is melted. Press through a strainer to remove bits of fruit.

Brush a thin layer of jam glaze over bottom of pastry. Then add a layer of apricots, cut side down; brush with more glaze. Arrange a second layer of apricots, cut side down, atop the first; brush generously with glaze. Sprinkle with almonds and brush with remaining glaze. Bake until crust is golden brown and apricots are heated through (about 15 minutes). Place on a rack and let cool; then remove pan sides. Makes about 8 servings.

Dutch Magic Tart

Line a tart pan with pastry, pour in cake batter, drizzle chocolate syrup atop—and like magic, the syrup sinks to form a fudgy layer under the cake.

         Sweet Butter Pastry for a 10-inch tart (page 8)
      1 cup all-purpose flour
     1½ teaspoons baking powder
      ¼ cup butter or margarine, softened
     1½ cups sugar
      1 egg
      1 teaspoon vanilla
      ½ cup milk
      ¼ cup sifted unsweetened cocoa
      6 tablespoons water
         Sweetened whipped cream or ice cream

Preheat oven to 350°. Roll out pastry and line a 10-inch fluted tart pan with a removable bottom as directed on page 41.

In a bowl, mix flour and baking powder. In another bowl, beat butter and 1 cup of the sugar until blended; beat in egg and ½ teaspoon of the vanilla. Add flour mixture to butter mixture alternately with milk; pour batter into pastry shell.

Stir together cocoa and remaining ½ cup sugar; stir in water and remaining ½ teaspoon vanilla until smooth. Pour evenly over batter. Bake until cake feels firm in center when lightly pressed (about 45 minutes). Place on a rack; let cool completely, then remove pan sides. Serve with whipped cream. Makes about 8 servings.

Blueberry-Lemon Tart

Smooth, tart lemon curd is a perfect foil for fresh blueberries. If you like, make both crust and filling in advance, then assemble and top with blueberries just before serving.

      Lemon Butter (recipe follows)
      Sweet Butter Pastry for a 10-inch tart (page 8)
2½ **to 3 cups blueberries**
      Powdered sugar

Prepare Lemon Butter and refrigerate.

Preheat oven to 350°. Roll out pastry and line a 10-inch fluted tart pan with a removable bottom as directed on page 41. Prick pastry all over with a fork. Bake in lower third of oven until golden brown (22 to 25 minutes). Place on a rack and let cool.

Spread Lemon Butter evenly in pastry shell; top evenly with blueberries. Serve; or refrigerate for up to 3 hours.

To serve, remove pan sides and dust tart generously with powdered sugar. Cut into wedges with a sharp knife. Makes 6 to 8 servings.

Lemon Butter. In top of a double boiler over simmering water, melt ¼ cup **butter** or margarine. Add ½ teaspoon grated **lemon peel,** ¼ cup **fresh lemon juice,** ½ cup plus 2 tablespoons **sugar,** and 2 **eggs;** stir with a wire whisk until blended. Cook, whisking constantly, until thickened and smooth. Let cool. Cover and refrigerate until cold (about 1 hour) or for up to 1 week.

Strawberry Oat Tart

Here's a quick-to-make summertime tart—it's like a big oatmeal cookie topped with vanilla custard and plump whole strawberries.

      Sweet Oatmeal Pastry for a 10 or 11-inch tart (page 8)
3 **egg yolks**
2 **teaspoons vanilla**
1 **tablespoon cornstarch**
3 **tablespoons sugar**
1 **cup milk**
4 **cups hulled strawberries**

Preheat oven to 375°. Roll out pastry and line a 10 or 11-inch fluted tart pan with a removable bottom as directed on page 41. Prick pastry all over with a fork. Bake in lower third of oven until golden brown (about 20 minutes). Place on a rack and let cool.

In a bowl, beat egg yolks and vanilla until well blended; set aside. In a 2 to 3-quart pan, stir together cornstarch and sugar. Gradually stir in milk; bring to a boil over medium-low heat, stirring constantly. Stir a small amount of the hot milk mixture into egg yolks; then stir egg mixture into pan, reduce heat to low, and stir constantly for 1 minute. Set pan in a bowl of ice water and stir to cool.

Spread custard in pastry shell; cover with strawberries, arranging them with pointed ends up. Remove pan sides. Makes about 8 servings.

Sweet Cherry Tart

A buttery pastry shell filled with sweet cherry purée and topped with glossy whole cherries makes a showpiece dessert.

      Lemon Pastry for an 11-inch tart (page 8)
6 **cups pitted dark sweet cherries**
½ **cup sugar**
2 **tablespoons cornstarch**
2 **tablespoons lemon juice**
⅛ **teaspoon ground cinnamon**
      Dash of salt
⅓ **cup red currant jelly**

Preheat oven to 350°. Roll out pastry and line an 11-inch fluted tart pan with a removable bottom as directed on page 41. Prick pastry all over with a fork. Bake in lower third of oven until golden brown (22 to 25 minutes). Let cool on a rack.

Select 4 cups of the prettiest cherries and set aside. Whirl remaining 2 cups cherries in a food processor or blender until smoothly puréed. In a 2-quart pan, combine sugar and cornstarch; stir in cherry purée, lemon juice, cinnamon, and salt. Cook over medium heat, stirring, until bubbly and thickened. Let cool slightly, then pour into pastry shell. Refrigerate until set (about 1 hour).

Arrange reserved 4 cups cherries evenly over filling. Place jelly in a small pan; stir over low heat until melted, then brush evenly over cherries. Refrigerate tart until glaze is set (about 15 minutes) or for up to 4 hours. Remove pan sides. Makes about 8 servings.

Raspberry Tartlets

1 Using back of a spoon, press raspberry pulp up against strainer sides to extract as much juice as possible; discard seeds.

2 Let shells cool completely on a rack. Invert each pan; gently tap bottom until pastry falls out into your hand. Turn right side up.

3 Cooked raspberry curd has the consistency of thick pudding; it firms up upon cooling.

4 To decorate, fill pastry bag with whipped cream. Holding twisted top in one hand, squeeze to release cream; guide tip with other hand.

Raspberry Tartlets

(Pictured on facing page)

For an elegant finale to a springtime luncheon, offer tartlets filled with delicate raspberry curd.

Sweet Butter Pastry for an 11-inch tart (page 8)
1 cup **fresh raspberries** (or unsweetened **frozen berries,** thawed and drained)
3 tablespoons **lemon juice**
½ cup (¼ lb.) **butter or margarine**
3 tablespoons **sugar**
4 **eggs**
Red food color (optional)
Sweetened whipped cream
Fresh raspberries or mint sprigs

Preheat oven to 350°. For the tartlet shells, you'll need 17 barquette or other tartlet pans, each with a volume of about 3 tablespoons. Place a rounded tablespoonful of pastry dough in each pan; press evenly over bottom and up sides of pan. Prick lightly with a fork. Bake until golden brown (15 to 20 minutes); place on a rack and let cool. Invert pans and tap bottoms to release shells.

In a food processor or blender, whirl the 1 cup raspberries and lemon juice until puréed; press through a strainer to remove seeds.

Melt butter in a 2 to 3-quart pan over medium heat; reduce heat to low, then add raspberry purée, sugar, and eggs. Cook until mixture is smooth and thickened (about 10 minutes), stirring constantly with a wire whisk. For a deeper color, whisk in food color, a few drops at a time, until mixture is the shade desired. Let cool; then cover and refrigerate until thickened (about 1½ hours) or for up to 1 week.

To assemble, spoon 2½ to 3 tablespoons of the raspberry curd into each tartlet shell; top with whipped cream and garnish with raspberries. Serve; or cover loosely and refrigerate for up to 6 hours. Makes 17.

Apricot Tartlets

Follow directions for **Raspberry Tartlets,** but substitute ½ cup **apricot purée** for raspberry purée: combine ½ cup halved, pitted **apricots,** 2 tablespoons **sugar,** and ⅓ cup **water** in a pan. Bring to a boil; reduce heat, cover, and simmer until fruit is tender (5 to 10 minutes). Drain fruit well, then whirl in a food processor or blender until smooth. Measure ½ cup purée. (Or simply whirl ¾ cup drained canned apricot halves in a food processor or blender until smooth.)

Add 1 teaspoon grated **orange peel** to cooked filling. Garnish tartlets with **sweetened whipped cream** and thin strips of **orange peel.**

Coconut Tart

(Pictured on page 94)

Cooking on the island of Guadeloupe has a tempting French accent, especially noticeable in pastry treats like this coconut-custard delicacy.

Orange Flaky Pastry (recipe follows)
2 **eggs**
½ cup **sugar**
¼ teaspoon **salt**
¼ cup **all-purpose flour**
2⅔ cups (about 7 oz.) **lightly packed sweetened flaked coconut**
½ cup **orange juice**
½ cup (¼ lb.) **butter or margarine,** melted
¼ cup **apple or guava jelly**

Preheat oven to 325°. Prepare pastry. Reserve ⅓ of pastry for lattice top; press remaining pastry evenly over bottom and up sides of a 10-inch fluted tart pan with a removable bottom. Trim off any excess pastry to make edges of crust even with pan rim, then prick lightly all over with a fork. Bake for 8 minutes; place on a rack.

Divide reserved pastry into 10 pieces; roll each into a 10-inch rope and set aside.

In a bowl, lightly beat eggs; stir in sugar, salt, and flour. Add coconut, orange juice, and butter; stir to blend. Pour into pastry shell. Make a woven or easy lattice top (see pages 12 and 13) from pastry ropes; trim ends of ropes even with pan rim.

Bake tart until pastry is golden brown (about 40 minutes). Transfer tart to a rack. Place jelly in a small pan and stir over low heat until melted; carefully brush over hot tart. Let cool for at least 12 hours before removing pan sides and cutting. Makes 10 to 12 servings.

Orange Flaky Pastry. In a bowl, stir together 1⅔ cups **all-purpose flour,** ⅓ cup **sugar,** 1 teaspoon **baking powder,** and ¼ teaspoon **salt.** Then stir in 1 teaspoon grated **orange peel.** With your fingers, work in ½ cup (¼ lb.) **butter** or margarine, softened, until mixture is well blended. Add 1 **egg;** stir with a fork until dough holds together.

Glazed Berry Tarts

Glazed berries shine atop a layer of cream cheese filling in these individual tarts. You can use just about any fresh berry you like, but the smaller varieties (such as blackberries and raspberries) make the prettiest looking tarts.

> **Sweet Butter Pastry for a 10-inch tart (page 8)**
> 2 **small packages (3 oz. *each*) cream cheese, softened**
> 2 **tablespoons powdered sugar**
> ½ **teaspoon grated lemon peel**
> 1 **tablespoon cherry-flavored liqueur or lemon juice**
> 2½ **cups blackberries, raspberries, or boysenberries**
> ½ **cup red currant jelly**

Preheat oven to 350°. For each tartlet, press a rounded tablespoonful of pastry dough evenly over bottom and sides of a 2½-inch fluted tart pan or muffin cup (measured across the top). Bake until golden (20 to 22 minutes). Place on a rack and let cool, then invert pans and tap bottoms to release pastry shells.

In a bowl, beat cream cheese and sugar until smooth. Beat in lemon peel and liqueur. Carefully spread about 1 tablespoon of the mixture in the bottom of each pastry shell. Top with berries, dividing fruit evenly among shells.

Place jelly in a small pan and stir over low heat until melted. Brush over each tart, covering berries generously. Refrigerate tarts, lightly covered, until glaze is set (at least 1 hour) or for up to 24 hours. Makes 12.

Lemon Velvet Tarts

Like cheesecake, these tiny tarts feature a lemony, velvety-smooth filling.

> **Flaky Pastry for a double-crust 9-inch pie (page 7)**
> 3 **eggs**
> ¾ **cup sugar**
> 2 **teaspoons grated lemon peel**
> ½ **cup fresh lemon juice**
> 1 **large package (8 oz.) cream cheese, softened**
> **Mint sprigs (optional)**

Preheat oven to 450°. On a lightly floured board, roll out pastry to a thickness of ⅛ inch. Cut into twelve 4½-inch circles (re-roll scraps and cut again if necessary).

Drape pastry circles over the bottoms of 3-inch muffin cups (measured across the top), alternating cups so pastry shells don't touch each other. Pleat pastry around cups; with a fork, prick bottom of each shell several times. Bake until golden brown (7 to 8 minutes). Let cool completely before removing from pans.

In top of a double boiler, beat eggs until well blended. Gradually add sugar, beating until mixture is pale in color and falls in a thick ribbon from beaters. Stir in lemon peel and lemon juice until blended. Cook over simmering water, stirring constantly, until custard has thickened enough to lightly coat a metal spoon (about 5 minutes). Remove from heat.

Cut cream cheese into 1-inch chunks; beat into custard, a few chunks at a time, until blended. Let filling cool, then spoon into pastry shells. Cover and refrigerate for up to 8 hours. If desired, garnish each tart with a mint sprig just before serving. Makes 12.

Mincemeat-Cheese Tarts

Homemade mincemeat tastes best in these tarts, but purchased mincemeat also works well—either the bottled ready-to-use type or the boxed condensed form, reconstituted according to package directions.

> **Flaky Pastry for a single-crust 9-inch pie (page 7)**
> 1 **small package (3 oz.) cream cheese, softened**
> 1 **tablespoon sugar**
> 1 **tablespoon brandy or apple juice**
> ½ **teaspoon grated orange peel**
> 1½ **cups mincemeat, homemade (page 24) or purchased**
> ⅓ **cup chopped nuts**

Preheat oven to 450°. On a lightly floured board, roll out pastry to a thickness of ⅛ inch. Cut into eight 4-inch circles (re-roll scraps and cut again if necessary).

Drape pastry circles over bottoms of 2½-inch muffin cups (measured across the top), alternating cups so pastry shells don't touch each other. Pleat pastry around cups; with a fork, prick bottom of each shell several times. Bake until golden brown

(7 to 8 minutes). Let cool completely before removing from pans.

In a bowl, beat cream cheese, sugar, brandy, and orange peel until smooth. Spoon an equal amount into each pastry shell. Stir together mincemeat and nuts; spoon about 3 tablespoons into each tart. Cover and refrigerate for at least 1 hour or up to 24 hours. Makes 8.

Almond Tartlets

Almond paste gives special richness to these bite-size tartlets. If you use canned almond paste, you'll have about half a can left over; you can freeze it, tightly wrapped, for up to 6 months.

- ½ cup almond paste
- ⅓ cup sugar
- 4 teaspoons butter or margarine, softened
- 1 teaspoon *each* vanilla and rum
- 2 eggs
  Orange Pastry for an 11-inch tart (page 8)
- ⅓ cup sliced almonds
- ⅓ cup apricot jam (optional)

In small bowl of an electric mixer, beat almond paste, sugar, butter, vanilla, rum, and eggs until smooth. Set aside.

Preheat oven to 350°. On a lightly floured board, roll out pastry to a thickness of ⅛ inch; cut into about thirty 2½-inch circles (re-roll scraps and cut again if necessary). Fit circles into tiny fluted tartlet pans or muffin cups (about 1¾ inches across the top). Spoon filling into tartlet shells; sprinkle a few almonds over each tartlet. Bake until filling is firm and pastry is lightly browned (10 to 12 minutes). Place on a rack; let cool for 10 minutes. Remove from pans.

If you want jam-glazed tartlets, place jam in a small pan and stir over low heat until melted. Press through a strainer to remove bits of fruit, then spoon over tartlets. Makes about 30.

Sugarless Apple Tarts

Apple juice concentrate supplies natural sweetness for the spiced apples that fill these tarts.

Flaky Pastry for a double-crust 9-inch pie (page 7)
- 1 can (12 oz.) frozen apple juice concentrate
- 2 tablespoons butter or margarine
- 3 tablespoons quick-cooking tapioca
- ⅛ teaspoon salt
- 1 teaspoon ground cinnamon
- ½ teaspoon ground nutmeg
- 6 to 7 cups peeled, thinly sliced tart green apples or Golden Delicious apples
  Sweetened whipped cream
- ½ cup sliced almonds

Preheat oven to 450°. On a lightly floured board, roll out pastry to a thickness of ⅛ inch. Cut into twelve 4½-inch circles (re-roll scraps and cut again if necessary). Drape pastry circles over the bottoms of 3-inch muffin cups (measured across the top), alternating cups so pastry shells don't touch each other. Pleat pastry around cups; with a fork, prick bottom of each shell several times. Bake until golden brown (7 to 8 minutes). Let cool completely before removing from pans.

In a wide frying pan, combine apple juice concentrate, butter, tapioca, salt, cinnamon, nutmeg, and apples. Bring to a boil; then reduce heat, cover, and simmer, stirring occasionally, until apples are tender (15 to 20 minutes). Let cool; cover and refrigerate for up to 2 days.

At serving time, spoon about ⅓ cup of the apple filling into each tart shell. Top each with a spoonful of whipped cream and about 2 teaspoons almonds. Makes 12.

Storing Tart Shells

Making tarts is extra easy when you keep baked pastry shells on hand, ready to fill and serve.

To store tartlet shells, remove cooled shells from pans; wrap airtight and store at room temperature for up to 2 days. For longer storage, pack shells in a rigid container, separating each layer of shells with wax paper; seal and freeze.

To store full-size shells, don't remove from pans; just wrap airtight and let stand for up to 2 days. Or freeze for longer storage.

Let frozen pastry shells stand at room temperature until thawed before filling.

Freezer Pies

Because busy cooks welcome ideas for cooking ahead, we've gathered a collection of impressive pies that need not be served the same day they're made. Unlike most pies, these frozen treats are long lived. They'll taste fresh for days, so they can be made well in advance—ready to pull from the freezer for a special company meal or a quick family dessert.

How long can you keep a freezer pie on hold? A month at the most—if the pie is kept longer, the texture may become grainy, the flavor flat. *Pies to be stored for any more than a day should be wrapped airtight.* Cover the top of the frozen pie loosely with foil and seal the edges over the pan rim; then slip the covered pie into a freezer bag, seal, and return to the freezer.

If you prefer, you can store the pie in individual servings—just cut the frozen pie into wedges, then wrap and freeze each slice separately.

Mocha Alaska Pie

Hidden under a mountain of snowy meringue is a coffee ice cream sundae capped with chocolate and nuts. Last-minute baking turns the pristine topping golden brown, but the filling stays firm and chilly.

- 1 quart coffee ice cream, softened
  Chocolate Crumb Crust for a 9-inch pie, baked and cooled (page 9)
- 1 can (5½ oz.) chocolate-flavored syrup
- ½ cup chopped walnuts or hazelnuts (filberts), toasted
- 3 egg whites (at room temperature)
- ¼ teaspoon cream of tartar
- 6 tablespoons sugar

Spread ice cream evenly in crust. Freeze until firm. Drizzle chocolate syrup over ice cream; sprinkle walnuts over syrup. Return to freezer.

In large bowl of an electric mixer, beat egg whites and cream of tartar until frothy. Add sugar, 1 tablespoon at a time, beating well after each addition. Continue to beat until sugar is dissolved and meringue holds glossy, stiff peaks.

Swirl meringue evenly over pie, sealing it to crust; return pie to freezer. When meringue is frozen, cover pie lightly and return to freezer. To store for more than 1 day, wrap airtight as directed at left.

To serve, preheat oven to 450°. Bake frozen pie, uncovered, until meringue is golden brown (about 4 minutes). Makes 6 to 8 servings.

Frozen Strawberry Cream Pie

(Pictured on facing page)

Capture the sweetness of plump ripe strawberries in this luscious pie, then tuck it away in your freezer for a special occasion. The extra-smooth meringue base is made from hot sugar syrup whipped into egg whites. To prevent spattering, pour the syrup onto the whipped whites near the side of the bowl, not directly onto the beaters.

- 2 tablespoons orange-flavored liqueur or 1 tablespoon lemon juice
- 3½ cups strawberries
- ¼ cup water
- 1 cup sugar
- 1 teaspoon light corn syrup
- 3 egg whites (at room temperature)
- 1½ cups whipping cream
  Vanilla Crumb Crust for a 9-inch springform pan, baked and cooled (page 9)

In a food processor or blender, whirl liqueur and 2 cups of the strawberries until puréed. Set aside.

In a 1-quart pan, combine water, sugar, and corn syrup; bring to a boil over medium heat, stirring until sugar is dissolved. Continue to cook until syrup reaches 240°F (soft ball stage) on a candy thermometer. Remove from heat.

At once place egg whites in large bowl of an electric mixer and beat until soft peaks form; slowly beat in hot syrup. Then beat on high speed until meringue has cooled to room temperature (6 to 8 minutes).

Fold berry purée into meringue. Whip cream until soft peaks form; gently fold into meringue. Turn mixture into crust; cover and freeze. To store for more than 1 day, wrap airtight as directed at left.

At serving time, remove pan sides; place pie on a platter. Cut remaining 1½ cups strawberries in half lengthwise; arrange in a ring around edge of pie. Let pie soften at room temperature for 15 minutes, then serve. Makes 8 to 10 servings.

Frozen Strawberry Cream Pie

1 Beat egg whites until they hold soft peaks. Slowly beat in hot syrup. Don't scrape syrup off pan sides into bowl—meringue might be grainy.

2 Beating the egg white-syrup mixture for 6 to 8 minutes produces a light, fluffy mixture that resembles marshmallow creme. The meringue mixture is fairly stiff at this stage.

3 Fold together berry purée and meringue: using spatula, cut down center and turn flat side of spatula toward you as you lift meringue up against side of bowl; repeat, turning bowl.

4 Pour strawberry fluff atop baked, cooled vanilla crumb crust. Using spatula, make top as smooth as possible. Cover and freeze until firm.

Frozen Brickle & Nut Pie

This pie will remind you of butter brickle ice cream. Both almond brickle bits and chopped almonds are stirred into the vanilla custard base.

>   2 **eggs (at room temperature), separated**
>   ½ **cup *each* milk and firmly packed brown sugar**
>   2 **teaspoons vanilla**
>   1 **cup whipping cream**
>   1 **package (7.8 oz.) or 1 can (9 oz.) almond brickle bits**
>   1½ **cups chopped blanched almonds**
>   **Graham Cracker Crust for a 9-inch pie, baked and cooled (page 9)**
>   **Grated bittersweet chocolate**

In a heavy 1-quart pan, combine egg yolks, milk, and sugar. Cook over medium-low heat, stirring constantly, until custard has thickened enough to lightly coat a metal spoon. Stir in 1 teaspoon of the vanilla. Pour into a shallow pan and let cool; then freeze until slushy (about 1 hour).

In a bowl, beat egg whites until they hold moist, stiff peaks. In another bowl, whip cream until it holds soft peaks. Stir remaining 1 teaspoon vanilla into cream, then fold cream into egg whites.

Stir partially frozen custard; fold into cream mixture, a spoonful at a time. Fold in brickle bits and almonds. Turn mixture into crust and sprinkle with chocolate; freeze solid. To store for more than 1 day, wrap airtight as directed on page 50.

Let pie soften at room temperature for 15 minutes before cutting. Makes 6 to 8 servings.

Frosty Lemon Pie

Though rich tasting and satisfying, this pie is surprisingly low in calories.

>   **Macaroon Crumb Crust (page 9)**
>   2 **eggs (at room temperature), separated**
>   ⅔ **cup sugar**
>   1 **teaspoon grated lemon peel**
>   ⅓ **cup fresh lemon juice**
>   **Dash of salt**
>   ⅔ **cup *each* instant nonfat dry milk and ice water**

Preheat oven to 350°. Press about ¾ of the crumb crust mixture over bottom of a 9-inch spring-form pan; set remainder aside. Bake crust until lightly browned (8 to 10 minutes). Place on a rack and let cool.

In small bowl of an electric mixer, beat egg yolks until foamy. Gradually add ½ cup of the sugar and continue to beat until mixture falls from beaters in a thick ribbon. Blend in lemon peel, lemon juice, and salt.

Wash and dry beaters. In large bowl of mixer, beat egg whites, dry milk, ice water, and remaining sugar on highest speed until mixture holds stiff peaks (about 5 minutes). Add yolk mixture and beat on lowest speed just until blended. Pour into crust and sprinkle with reserved crumb mixture; freeze solid. To store for more than 1 day, wrap airtight as directed on page 50.

Remove pan sides and let pie soften at room temperature for 15 minutes before cutting. Makes 6 to 8 servings.

Pumpkin Ice Cream Pie

This refreshing pie is a perfect ending for summer barbecues and holiday meals alike.

>   1 **pint vanilla ice cream, softened**
>   **Gingersnap Crumb Crust for a 9-inch pie, baked and cooled (page 9)**
>   ¾ **cup sugar**
>   ¼ **teaspoon salt**
>   ½ **teaspoon *each* ground nutmeg, ginger, and cinnamon**
>   1 **cup canned pumpkin**
>   1 **cup whipping cream**
>   **Caramel Sauce (optional; page 57)**

Spread ice cream evenly over bottom of crust. Place in freezer.

In a 2-quart pan, stir together sugar, salt, nutmeg, ginger, and cinnamon. Stir in pumpkin. Cook over medium heat, stirring occasionally, until sugar is dissolved and mixture is warm to the touch. Remove from heat and let cool.

Whip cream until it holds soft peaks; gently fold into pumpkin mixture. Spoon into ice-cream-lined crust; freeze solid. To store for more than 1 day, wrap airtight as directed on page 50.

Let pie soften at room temperature for 15 minutes before cutting. Pass Caramel Sauce to top each slice, if desired. Makes 6 to 8 servings.

Berry Ripple Ice Cream Pie

This impressive dessert is simply a dressed-up version of an old favorite: berries and ice cream. The pie is filled with layers of vanilla ice cream and raspberry or strawberry sauce, then topped with a fluffy marshmallow meringue.

Sweet Butter Pastry for a single-crust 9-inch pie (page 8)
Cooked Berry Sauce (recipe follows)
1 quart vanilla ice cream, softened
3 egg whites (at room temperature)
1 cup marshmallow creme
1 teaspoon vanilla
Fresh Berry Sauce (recipe follows)

Preheat oven to 325°. Press pastry over bottom and up sides of a 9-inch pie pan. Bake until light golden brown (25 to 30 minutes); place on a rack and let cool. Prepare Cooked Berry Sauce; let cool, then cover and refrigerate until cold.

Spread about ⅓ of the ice cream in crust, then cover with about half the cooked sauce. Repeat layers, ending with ice cream. Freeze solid.

In large bowl of an electric mixer, beat egg whites until they hold soft peaks. Beat in marshmallow creme, a large spoonful at a time, until meringue holds peaks that curl slightly when beaters are withdrawn. Blend in vanilla. Swirl meringue over pie, sealing it to crust; return pie to freezer. When meringue is frozen, cover pie; return to freezer. To store for more than 1 day, wrap airtight as directed on page 50.

Prepare Fresh Berry Sauce; cover and refrigerate. Preheat oven to 450°. Bake frozen pie, uncovered, until meringue is golden brown (about 4 minutes). Pass Fresh Berry Sauce to top each slice of pie. Makes 6 to 8 servings.

Cooked Berry Sauce. In a small pan, stir together 1½ cups fresh **raspberries** or strawberries, 6 tablespoons **sugar,** and 1½ tablespoons **cornstarch.** Then stir in 4½ tablespoons **water** and 3 tablespoons **light corn syrup.** Cook over medium heat, stirring and mashing berries with a spoon, until mixture boils and thickens. Remove from heat and add 1 tablespoon **lemon juice.**

Fresh Berry Sauce. In a blender or food processor, whirl 2 cups fresh **raspberries** or strawberries until puréed. Stir in ⅓ cup **sugar** and 1 cup fresh whole **raspberries** or sliced strawberries.

Peach-Yogurt Pie

Make this refreshing summer pie when peaches are at their peak of juicy sweetness.

1 large package (8 oz.) cream cheese, softened
1 carton (8 oz.) peach-flavored yogurt
⅓ cup instant nonfat dry milk
½ cup honey or sugar
1½ cups coarsely chopped peaches
Macaroon Crumb Crust for a 9-inch pie, baked and cooled (page 9)
2 cups sliced peaches, sweetened to taste

In a food processor or blender, whirl cream cheese, yogurt, dry milk, and honey until smooth. Add chopped peaches; whirl just until blended. Spoon into crust and freeze solid. To store for more than 1 day, wrap airtight as directed on page 50.

Let pie soften at room temperature for 15 minutes before cutting; top each serving with sliced peaches. Makes 6 to 8 servings.

Chocolate Mint Pie

Two rich chocolate layers surround a vanilla ice cream center marbled with crème de menthe.

⅔ cup butter or margarine, softened
1⅓ cups powdered sugar
2 eggs
2 ounces unsweetened chocolate, melted and cooled
Chocolate Crumb Crust for a 9-inch pie, baked and cooled (page 9)
2 tablespoons green crème de menthe
1½ pints vanilla ice cream, softened
¼ cup finely chopped walnuts

In large bowl of an electric mixer, beat butter and sugar until creamy. Add eggs, one at a time, and beat until fluffy. Blend in chocolate. Spread half the mixture over crust; freeze solid.

Swirl crème de menthe through ice cream. Evenly spread over chocolate layer. Freeze solid. Spread remaining chocolate mixture over ice cream. Sprinkle with walnuts; again freeze solid. To store for more than 1 day, wrap airtight as directed on page 50. Makes 8 to 10 servings.

Kolache

1 On a lightly floured board, roll out dough to a 12 by 16-inch rectangle. With a sharp knife, cut dough into 4-inch squares; remove excess dough.

2 For closed turnovers, spread filling in a triangle over half of square; moisten edges with water. Fold other half of square over filling; lightly press edges together with fingers.

3 To seal edges, press firmly with back of a floured fork. Cut small slashes in top of turnover to allow steam to escape. Place on an ungreased baking sheet.

4 For open turnovers, place filling in a diagonal strip across square. Fold opposite corners of square to center; moisten with water and press to seal.

Turnovers

We think of turnovers as the most portable of pies, perfect for picnics or any other time you want a sweet which can be eaten out of hand. Flaky pastry works well for these treats, but if you prefer a sweeter wrapper, try the soft cream cheese dough we use for our *kolache.*

When you fill turnovers, don't be too generous —an overstuffed turnover will come unsealed as it bakes, and the filling will leak out.

Kolache

(Pictured on facing page)

You can shape these pastries two ways. Fold each dough square in half, completely enclosing the filling; or use a "blanket" wrap, so filling peeks out.

    1 cup (½ lb.) butter or margarine, softened
    1 large package (8 oz.) cream cheese, softened
       About ½ cup sugar
    1 teaspoon vanilla
    2 eggs
    3 cups all-purpose flour
    1 teaspoon baking powder
    ½ teaspoon salt
       Apricot or Prune Filling (recipe follows)

In large bowl of an electric mixer, beat butter, cream cheese, and ½ cup of the sugar until creamy. Beat in vanilla. Add eggs, one at a time, beating well after each addition. Stir together flour, baking powder, and salt; gradually beat into butter mixture until dough is blended. Divide dough in half, wrap each portion in plastic wrap, and refrigerate until firm (at least 3 hours). Meanwhile, prepare filling of your choice.

Preheat oven to 325°. On a lightly floured board, roll out one portion of dough to a 12 by 16-inch rectangle; cut into 4-inch squares. Spread filling in a triangle on half of each square to within ½ inch of edges; dampen edges, fold other half over, and press edges with a fork to seal. (Or spread a scant tablespoon of filling on each square, in a diagonal strip extending to within ¼ inch of 2 opposite corners. Fold other 2 corners to middle, overlapping them; moisten with water and press gently to seal.) Repeat rolling and filling with remaining dough.

Sprinkle kolache very lightly with sugar; place slightly apart on ungreased baking sheets. Bake until edges are lightly browned (22 to 25 minutes). Place on a rack; let cool. Makes 24.

Apricot or Prune Filling. Place 1 cup **dried apricots** or pitted prunes in a small pan; add ½ cup **water,** ¾ cup **sugar,** ½ teaspoon grated **lemon peel,** 1 tablespoon **lemon juice,** ¼ teaspoon **ground cinnamon,** and ⅛ teaspoon **ground cloves.** Bring to a boil over medium heat; reduce heat, cover, and simmer until fruit is tender (10 to 15 minutes).

Remove from heat and let cool for 10 minutes; then whirl in a blender or food processor until smooth. (You should have about 1¼ cups. If necessary, cook and stir over low heat to reduce to 1¼ cups; or add water to make 1¼ cups.) Let cool.

Apple Turnovers

Finely chopped walnuts secured by a lemon glaze give these turnovers a professional look.

    ⅓ cup walnut pieces
    3 cups finely chopped tart green apples
    ⅓ cup granulated sugar
    ½ teaspoon ground cinnamon
    ¼ teaspoon ground nutmeg
    4 teaspoons lemon juice
       Flaky Pastry for a double-crust
       9-inch pie (page 7)
    ½ cup powdered sugar

Preheat oven to 425°. Finely chop half the walnuts; set aside. Coarsely chop remaining walnuts; place in a bowl and stir in apples, granulated sugar, cinnamon, nutmeg, and 1 teaspoon of the lemon juice. Stir well.

Cut pastry into 8 equal pieces. Shape each piece into a ball; on a floured board, roll out each ball to a 7-inch circle. For each turnover, moisten edges of one circle with water. Place about ⅓ cup of the apple filling on half of circle, spreading it to ½ inch of edges; fold other half over to enclose. Press edges with a fork to seal; slash top. Place turnovers 1 inch apart on an ungreased baking sheet. Bake until golden brown (20 to 25 minutes).

Stir together powdered sugar and remaining 3 teaspoons lemon juice. Place hot baked turnovers on a rack; brush with lemon glaze, then immediately sprinkle with finely chopped walnuts. Makes 8.

Meringue Shell Pies

A meringue's texture depends on the amount of sugar whipped into the egg whites. A relatively low ratio of sugar to egg whites results in a soft, fluffy meringue, like the topping that adorns a cream pie; a higher proportion of sugar yields a stiff, thick mixture known as *hard* meringue. Swirled in a pie pan and baked, a hard meringue makes a light, crisp shell that's an ideal container for custard or chiffon fillings, whipped cream, or fruit. (Don't worry if the shell cracks slightly as it cools—this is normal.)

Meringue shells also offer the advantage of make-ahead preparation: you can store the baked, cooled shells airtight at room temperature for up to 2 days.

For meringue with maximum volume, use large eggs, and have whites at room temperature before you beat them. (To bring whole eggs to room temperature quickly, cover them with warm water and let stand for 15 minutes.)

Angel Pie

It's easy to see why "angel" is used to describe many meringue shell pies—the filling softens the snowy shell, giving it a heavenly lightness.

  4 eggs (at room temperature), separated
  ½ teaspoon cream of tartar
  1½ cups sugar
  2 teaspoons grated lemon peel
  3 tablespoons fresh lemon juice
  1 cup whipping cream

Preheat oven to 275°. Butter a 9-inch pie pan. In large bowl of an electric mixer, beat egg whites and cream of tartar until frothy. Add 1 cup of the sugar, 1 tablespoon at a time, beating well after each addition. Continue to beat until sugar is dissolved and meringue holds glossy, stiff peaks.

Spread meringue in prepared pan, pushing it high on pan sides so it resembles a pie shell. Bake until lightly browned and dry to the touch (about 50 minutes). Place on a rack and let cool.

Place egg yolks in top of a double boiler. Beat with a wire whisk until blended, then whisk in remaining ½ cup sugar until dissolved. Stir in lemon peel and lemon juice. Cook over simmer-ing water, stirring constantly, until custard has thickened enough to lightly coat a metal spoon. (Custard will thicken further upon cooling.) Immediately remove from heat and replace water in bottom of double boiler with cold water. Stir custard over cold water until lukewarm, then cover and refrigerate until cold.

Whip cream until it holds soft peaks; fold chilled custard into cream. Turn filling into meringue shell. Refrigerate for at least 2 hours or up to 24 hours before serving. Makes 6 to 8 servings.

Cherry Angel Pie

Purchased cherry pie filling speeds the assembly of this pretty dessert, but its wonderful flavor is strictly "made from scratch."

  2 eggs (at room temperature), separated
  ¼ teaspoon cream of tartar
  1 cup sugar
  1 envelope unflavored gelatin
  ¼ cup cold water
  2 cups small curd cottage cheese
  ½ teaspoon grated lemon peel
  2 tablespoons fresh lemon juice
  1 can (21 oz.) cherry pie filling

Preheat oven to 275°. Butter a 9-inch pie pan. In large bowl of an electric mixer, beat egg whites and cream of tartar until frothy. Add ½ cup of the sugar, 1 tablespoon at a time, beating well after each addition. Continue to beat until sugar is dissolved and meringue holds glossy, stiff peaks.

Spread meringue in prepared pan, pushing it high on pan sides so it resembles a pie shell. Bake until lightly browned and dry to the touch (about 50 minutes). Place on a rack and let cool.

In a 1-quart pan, sprinkle gelatin over water and let soften for several minutes. Add remaining ½ cup sugar; stir over low heat until gelatin and sugar are dissolved. Remove from heat.

In a food processor or blender, whirl cottage cheese, lemon peel, lemon juice, and egg yolks until smooth; add gelatin mixture and whirl until combined. Refrigerate until mixture mounds slightly when dropped from a spoon, then turn into meringue shell; refrigerate until set. Spoon cherry pie filling over top; refrigerate for at least 2 hours or up to 24 hours before serving. Makes 6 to 8 servings.

Caramel Nut Angel Pie

This show-stopping dessert obligingly waits in the freezer for a special occasion.

- 2 **egg whites (at room temperature)**
- ¼ **cup sugar**
- 1½ **cups finely chopped almonds**
- ½ **gallon chocolate or coffee ice cream, softened**
- **Caramel Sauce (recipe follows)**

Preheat oven to 400°. Butter a 9-inch pie pan. In large bowl of an electric mixer, beat egg whites until frothy. Add sugar, 1 tablespoon at a time, beating well after each addition. Continue to beat until sugar is dissolved and meringue holds glossy, stiff peaks. Fold in almonds. Spread meringue in prepared pan, pushing it high on pan sides so it resembles a pie shell. Bake until lightly browned (about 10 minutes). Place on a rack and let cool.

Swirl ice cream into meringue shell. Freeze solid. To store for more than 1 day, wrap airtight as directed on page 50 (pie will keep for up to 1 month).

Prepare Caramel Sauce. Remove pie from freezer 10 minutes before cutting; top each slice with warm sauce. Makes 6 to 8 servings.

Caramel Sauce. Melt ¼ cup **butter** or margarine in a 1-quart pan over medium heat. Stir in 1 cup firmly packed **brown sugar;** cook, stirring, until dissolved. Stir in ½ cup **half-and-half** (light cream); cook and stir for 1 minute. Stir in ¼ cup chopped **almonds** and 1 teaspoon **vanilla.** Makes 1 cup.

Brownie Mint Pie

Cool mint cream fills a chewy, chocolaty shell.

- 18 **round chocolate cookie wafers (2¼ inches in diameter), finely crushed**
- ½ **cup walnuts, finely chopped**
- 3 **egg whites (at room temperature)**
- ¼ **teaspoon cream of tartar**
- ¾ **cup sugar**
- ½ **teaspoon vanilla**
- 1 **cup whipping cream**
- ¼ **cup crushed peppermint stick candy**
- **Semisweet chocolate curls (page 40)**

Preheat oven to 325°. Butter a 9-inch pie pan. In a bowl, combine cookie crumbs and walnuts; set aside.

In large bowl of an electric mixer, beat egg whites and cream of tartar until frothy. Add sugar, 1 tablespoon at a time, beating well after each addition. Continue to beat until sugar is dissolved and meringue holds glossy, stiff peaks. Blend in vanilla, then fold in crumb mixture.

Spread meringue in prepared pan, pushing it high on pan sides so it resembles a pie shell. Bake until meringue is dry to the touch (about 30 minutes). Place on a rack and let cool.

Whip cream until it holds soft peaks; fold in peppermint candy and spoon into meringue shell. Refrigerate for at least 3 hours or up to 24 hours; top with chocolate curls just before serving. Makes 6 to 8 servings.

Peanut Pie

When you have a craving for peanuts, try this pie. The meringue shell is packed with toasted nut flavor.

- ¾ **cup salted peanuts, finely chopped**
- 20 **round butter crackers (1¾ inches in diameter), finely crushed**
- **About 1 cup sugar**
- 3 **egg whites (at room temperature)**
- ¼ **teaspoon cream of tartar**
- 1 **cup whipping cream**
- ½ **teaspoon vanilla**

Preheat oven to 325°. Butter a 9-inch pie pan. Reserve 1 tablespoon of the peanuts; place remaining peanuts in a bowl and stir in cracker crumbs and ½ cup of the sugar. Set aside.

In large bowl of an electric mixer, beat egg whites and cream of tartar until frothy. Add ½ cup of the sugar, 1 tablespoon at a time, beating well after each addition. Continue to beat until sugar is dissolved and meringue holds glossy, stiff peaks. Fold peanut mixture into meringue.

Spread meringue in prepared pan, pushing it high on pan sides so it resembles a pie shell. Bake until dry to the touch (about 30 minutes). Place on a rack and let cool.

Whip cream until it holds soft peaks; beat in vanilla and sugar to taste. Turn into meringue shell and sprinkle with reserved peanuts. Serve, or refrigerate for up to 24 hours. Makes 6 servings.

Cheesecakes & Pies

It's the pan that makes the difference. That's one way to distinguish between cheese pie and cheesecake. Either can be light or incredibly rich; either can be smooth and creamy, dense or fluffy textured. And common to both is the use of a mild cheese, such as cream, Neufchâtel, or ricotta.

Cheese pie is usually cradled in a pie pan lined with a crumb crust. Cheesecake, on the other hand, is made with a crumb or pastry crust and baked in a spring-form (cheesecake) pan—a round pan with removable sides. Once you've removed the pan sides, you can transfer the chilled cake to a pretty plate or pedestal stand for a dramatic presentation. (Spring-form pans range from 8 to 12 inches across; they're sold in department stores and specialty cookware shops.)

Grand Old-fashioned Cheesecake

(Pictured on facing page)

This rich and elegant cheesecake is reminiscent of the one Grandma made with her own fresh cream cheese. The velvety filling is crowned with a smooth sour cream topping; your choice of raspberry or blueberry sauce dresses up each slice.

Both fresh and packaged cream cheese work well in this recipe (you'll find the fresh cheese sold in bulk at delicatessens, cheese shops, and some supermarkets and natural food stores). For easiest mixing, let the cheese—whether bulk or packaged—stand at room temperature until very soft before you make the filling.

Butter Pastry (recipe follows)
2½ pounds fresh cream cheese or 5 large packages (8 oz. *each*) cream cheese, softened
1½ cups plus 3 tablespoons sugar
6 eggs
¼ cup all-purpose flour
2 teaspoons grated lemon peel
½ teaspoon *each* salt and ground nutmeg
4 teaspoons vanilla
½ cup whipping cream
Raspberry Sauce or Blueberry Sauce (recipes follow)
1½ cups sour cream

Preheat oven to 400°. Prepare pastry; press ⅓ of the dough over bottom of a 10-inch spring-form pan with sides removed. Bake until pale golden (5 to 6 minutes); place on a rack and let cool. Butter pan sides, attach to pan bottom, and press remaining dough against sides to within ¼ inch of rim. Set aside. Reduce oven heat to 325°.

In large bowl of an electric mixer, beat cream cheese and 1½ cups of the sugar until soft and smooth; then beat in eggs, one at a time. Add flour, lemon peel, salt, nutmeg, and 3 teaspoons of the vanilla; beat just until smooth (do not overbeat). Stir in whipping cream. Pour filling into prepared crust and bake in a 325° oven until a knife inserted halfway to center comes out clean—1¼ to 1½ hours. (Check after 1 hour; if top is turning too brown, cover loosely with foil.)

While cake bakes, prepare sauce of your choice; let cool, then cover and refrigerate. Stir together sour cream, remaining 3 tablespoons sugar, and remaining 1 teaspoon vanilla; set aside.

As soon as cake is done, spread sour cream mixture over top; return cake to oven. Turn off oven and leave door ajar several inches. Let cheesecake remain in cooling oven for 1 hour, then place on a rack. Let cool for 15 minutes; loosen crust from pan sides with a knife, then let cake cool to room temperature. Cover and refrigerate for up to 2 days.

To serve, remove pan sides and place cake on a platter; pass sauce to top each slice. Makes about 20 servings.

Butter Pastry. In a food processor, whirl 1½ cups **all-purpose flour,** 3 tablespoons **sugar,** and ½ teaspoon grated **lemon peel** just until combined. Add ⅔ cup cold **butter** or margarine, cut into chunks; whirl until crumbs the size of small peas form. Add 1 **egg** and ¼ teaspoon **vanilla;** whirl until mixture begins to clump together (don't let it form a ball). Gather dough into a ball with your hands.

Raspberry Sauce. Thaw 3 packages (12 oz. *each*) **frozen lightly sweetened raspberries.** Press through a wire strainer set over a 2-quart pan. To juice in pan, add 3 tablespoons **light corn syrup;** 1½ tablespoons *each* **cornstarch** and **water** (stirred together); and ¾ cup **sugar.** Bring to a boil over medium heat, stirring; boil for 2 minutes. Remove from heat and let cool.

Blueberry Sauce. In a 2-quart pan, combine ⅓ cup **sugar** and 1 tablespoon **cornstarch.** Add ⅓ cup **water** and stir until smooth. Add 2 cups **fresh blueberries** (or frozen unsweetened berries, thawed) and 2 tablespoons **lemon juice.** Cook over medium heat, stirring, until mixture boils and thickens. Remove from heat and let cool.

Grand Old-fashioned Cheesecake

1 Press ⅓ of dough over bottom of a spring-form pan with sides removed. Bake until pale golden (pre-baking prevents crust from becoming soggy).

2 Let crust cool; then butter pan sides and attach to bottom. Press remaining dough evenly over sides to ¼ inch of rim. Smooth seam between baked bottom and unbaked sides.

3 For a velvety smooth filling, let cream cheese stand until very soft before blending with other ingredients. Pour filling into prepared crust; smooth out top. Bake on center oven rack.

4 Mix topping ingredients while cheesecake bakes—this gives sugar time to dissolve, making mixture extra smooth. Spread over hot cake.

Honey Cream Cheesecake

In this smooth and satisfying cheesecake, cream cheese is sweetened with thick, aromatic honey. Cups of hot spiced tea perfectly complement the cake's flavor.

    2 large packages (8 oz. *each*) cream cheese,
       softened
    2 eggs
    2 teaspoons vanilla
    ⅔ cup honey
       Graham Cracker Crust for a 9 or 10-inch
       spring-form pan, baked and cooled (page 9)
    2 cups sour cream

Preheat oven to 325°. In large bowl of an electric mixer, beat cream cheese until smooth. Add eggs, vanilla, and ⅓ cup of the honey; beat until well blended. Pour into crust. Bake until filling appears set in center when pan is gently shaken (about 25 minutes).

Stir together sour cream and ¼ cup of the remaining honey; spread evenly over cake and continue to bake until topping is set (5 to 6 more minutes). Place on a rack and let cool to room temperature; then cover and refrigerate for up to 2 days. To serve, remove pan sides and place cake on a plate. Drizzle remaining honey over top. Makes 10 servings.

Amaretto Cheesecake

Saluté to an incredibly smooth cheesecake! The unusual baking technique produces its silky texture. The crust is made with *amaretti,* the crisp Italian macaroons that come wrapped in tissue paper and packed in colorful cans.

       Almond Crust (recipe follows)
    3 large packages (8 oz. *each*) cream cheese,
       softened
   1⅓ cups sugar
    4 eggs
    ½ teaspoon grated lemon peel
    2 tablespoons lemon juice
    3 tablespoons amaretto or 1 teaspoon almond
       extract
    1 teaspoon vanilla
    ½ cup *each* whipping cream and sour cream

Preheat oven to 325°. Line bottom of a 5 by 9-inch loaf pan with wax paper; butter paper and pan sides. Prepare Almond Crust; press over bottom and 1 inch up sides of pan.

In large bowl of an electric mixer, beat cream cheese and sugar until well blended. Add eggs, one at a time, beating well after each addition. With mixer on lowest speed, beat in lemon peel, lemon juice, amaretto, vanilla, whipping cream, and sour cream. Pour into pan; place in a larger pan and pour in boiling water to a depth of 1 inch.

Bake until filling appears set in center when pan is gently shaken (1¼ to 1½ hours). Place on a rack and let cool for at least 3 hours. Invert onto a platter; peel off paper, then cover and refrigerate until completely cold (at least 5 hours) or for up to 2 days. Makes 12 servings.

Almond Crust. Finely crush enough **crisp almond macaroons** (about 2 cups) to make ¾ cup crumbs. Place in a bowl. Finely grind ½ cup whole **almonds;** add to crumbs, then stir in 3 tablespoons **butter** or margarine, melted.

Ricotta Rum Pie

This creamy cheese pie is similar to *cannoli.*

       Flaky Pastry for a single-crust 10-inch pie
       (page 7)
    2 pounds ricotta cheese
   1¼ cups powdered sugar
    ¼ teaspoon *each* salt, ground nutmeg, and
       ground cinnamon
    1 teaspoon vanilla
    ½ cup semisweet chocolate chips, chopped
    ½ cup chopped citron
    1 cup whipping cream
    ½ teaspoon rum flavoring

Preheat oven to 450°. Following directions on pages 12 and 13, roll out pastry, line a 10-inch pie pan, and bake blind. Place on a rack and let cool.

In large bowl of an electric mixer, beat ricotta cheese until smooth; beat in 1 cup of the sugar, salt, nutmeg, cinnamon, and vanilla. Stir in chocolate and citron. Cover and refrigerate for 1 hour, then turn into pastry shell.

Whip cream until it holds soft peaks; blend in remaining ¼ cup sugar and rum flavoring, then swirl over pie. Serve, or refrigerate for up to 12 hours. Makes 8 to 10 servings.

Yogurt Cheese Pie

A topping of sweetened fresh raspberries brightens each wedge of this tangy pie.

    Graham Cracker Crust (page 9)
- 1 **large package (8 oz.) cream cheese, softened**
- ½ **cup sugar**
- 3 **eggs**
- 2 **teaspoons vanilla**
- ¼ **teaspoon salt**
- 2 **cups plain yogurt**
- 2 **cups raspberries, sliced nectarines, or sliced peaches, sweetened to taste**

Preheat oven to 350°. Press crumb crust mixture over bottom and up sides of a 10-inch pie pan (crust will be fairly thin). Bake for 7 minutes; place on a rack and let cool.

In large bowl of an electric mixer, beat cream cheese and sugar until smooth. Beat in eggs, one at a time; then beat in vanilla and salt. With mixer on lowest speed, beat in yogurt just until blended.

Pour filling into crust. Bake until top feels dry when lightly touched and filling jiggles only slightly in center when pan is gently shaken (35 to 40 minutes). Place on a rack and let cool, to room temperature; then refrigerate for at least 4 hours or up to 24 hours. Spoon raspberries and any juices over each slice of pie. Makes 8 to 10 servings.

Chocolate Cheesecake

Whipped cream and a brown sugar meringue give this pale chocolate cheesecake its fluffy texture.

- 1½ **large packages (8 oz.** *each***) cream cheese, softened**
- 2 **eggs (at room temperature), separated**
- 1 **cup firmly packed light brown sugar**
- 1 **package (6 oz.) semisweet chocolate chips, melted and cooled**
- 1½ **cups whipping cream**
- 2 **tablespoons orange-flavored liqueur or brandy**
    Chocolate Crumb Crust for a 9 or 10-inch spring-form pan, baked and cooled (page 9)

In large bowl of an electric mixer, beat cream cheese until smooth. Add egg yolks and ½ cup of the sugar; beat until light and fluffy. With mixer on lowest speed, beat in chocolate.

Wash and dry beaters. In a bowl, beat egg whites until frothy. Add remaining ½ cup sugar, 1 tablespoon at a time, beating well after each addition. Continue to beat until sugar is dissolved and meringue holds glossy, stiff peaks. In another bowl, whip cream until it holds stiff peaks; blend in liqueur. Fold meringue and half the whipped cream into cheese mixture; turn into crust. Carefully spread remaining whipped cream over top. Cover and freeze until firm; remove pan sides before cutting. Makes 12 servings.

Danish Cheesecake

As this creamy cheesecake cools, a neat hollow forms in the top to hold the almond topping.

- ½ **cup (¼ lb.) butter or margarine, softened**
- 2 **large packages (8 oz.** *each***) cream cheese or Neufchâtel cheese, softened**
- 4 **eggs (at room temperature), separated**
- 1 **cup sugar**
- 1 **tablespoon cornstarch**
- 1 **teaspoon** *each* **baking powder, grated lemon peel, lemon juice, and vanilla**
    Zwieback Crumb Crust for a 9 or 10-inch spring-form pan, baked and cooled (page 9)
    Almond Topping (recipe follows)

Preheat oven to 325°. In large bowl of an electric mixer, beat butter and cream cheese until blended. Add egg yolks and beat until creamy. Beat in sugar, cornstarch, baking powder, lemon peel, lemon juice, and vanilla.

Wash and dry beaters. In a bowl, beat egg whites until they hold short, distinct peaks. Fold egg whites into cheese mixture; then turn into crust. Bake until filling feels set in center when lightly touched (50 to 60 minutes).

Immediately prepare Almond Topping and drizzle evenly over hot cake; place cake on a rack and let cool for 2 hours, then refrigerate for up to 2 days. Remove pan sides before serving. Makes 12 servings.

Almond Topping. Melt ¼ cup **butter** or margarine in a small pan over medium heat. Add ½ cup sliced **almonds;** stir until lightly toasted. Stir in ½ cup **sugar** and 3 tablespoons **whipping cream.** Bring to a boil; boil, stirring, for 1 minute.

Sweet Pastries

A pie has a typical shape—round—and a typical crust—flaky pastry. But what's a "typical" sweet pastry? There are dozens to choose from: creamy, chocolate-topped éclairs; elegant napoleons; crisp apple strudel and honey-drenched *baklava;* buttery croissants and bear claws. Shapes, sizes, and basic doughs all differ.

Despite their great variety, a few common threads draw all these pastries together. The dough forms a container or base for a sweet filling—sometimes rich and elaborate, sometimes just a sprinkling of sugar or nuts. And the doughs we use also have an underlying similarity. All are based on the same three ingredients: flour, fat, and liquid.

Four basic doughs. See-through *fila* is the simplest pastry dough, made only from flour, fat, and water. Stacked and rolled or folded, it's used for Middle Eastern delicacies as well as European strudel.

Glorious *puff pastry* gets its multilayered, shattery-crisp texture from a very high proportion of butter to flour. It's the base for classic sweets such as cream horns and napoleons—and for simple delights like sugar-crusted *palmiers.*

The addition of *yeast* to the basic ingredients yields a supple, spongy dough that can be twisted into all sorts of shapes. Layered

with butter, it makes flaky croissants; wrapped around a filling, it produces tender Danishes and coffeecakes.

Eggs and additional liquid are stirred into the basic mix for *chou paste,* perhaps the most versatile dough of all. You can spoon or pipe it into puffs, fingers, or rings; all bake into crisp, hollow shells, ready to hold any filling.

Ready-made convenience. While freshly made puff pastry and fila (strudel) dough are among the crowning achievements of any baker, they're also difficult and time-consuming for the home cook to prepare. Fortunately, though, both can be purchased in most supermarkets. Using prepared fila or puff pastry, you can complete special desserts in record time—just add a homemade filling or topping.

Basic simplicity. In this chapter, we've included some of the most celebrated creations in the world of baking. A few may seem dauntingly elaborate, but even the most complex pastry is just a combination of basic recipes. *Gâteau St.-Honoré,* for example, is nothing more than a round of buttery short pastry, ringed with small cream puffs and filled with a mixture of pastry cream and whipped cream.

In addition to making fancy desserts seem more approachable, breaking a recipe down into basic elements helps you plan advance preparation. Even if a dish tastes best if assembled just before serving, its components can often be completed hours or days in advance.

Lovely to look at, exquisite to eat—and easy to make. The recipe for Napoleons is on page 76.

Fila Dough

Fila is a transparent, tissue-thin dough that forms the foundation for a variety of delicacies, from Balkan *baklava* to Hungarian strudel. It's sold fresh or frozen, in 1-pound packages; you may see it labeled filo, fillo, phyllo, or strudel leaves. Each package contains about 25 sheets of dough, each about 12 by 16 inches.

Greek Milk Pie

Sweet confections made with delicate fila dough line the shelves of pastry shops in Greece. One of the most popular is this not-too-sweet custard dessert—*galatoboureko*, or milk pie.

 8 eggs (at room temperature)
 1 cup sugar
 1½ cups farina (regular cream-of-wheat cereal)
 8 cups milk
 1½ teaspoons grated lemon peel
 4 teaspoons vanilla
 ½ teaspoon ground nutmeg
 ¼ teaspoon salt
 2 tablespoons butter or margarine
 1 package (1 lb.) fila (thawed if frozen)
 ⅔ cup butter or margarine, melted
 Cinnamon Syrup (recipe follows)

Place eggs and sugar in a 4 to 5-quart pan; beat with an electric mixer on high speed until mixture is thick and lemon colored. Gradually beat in farina and milk. Cook over medium-high heat, stirring, until steaming (about 8 minutes). Reduce heat to medium-low. Continue to cook, stirring often, until mixture has the consistency of porridge (10 to 15 more minutes).

Remove from heat; stir in lemon peel, vanilla, nutmeg, salt, and the 2 tablespoons butter. Cover with plastic wrap, pressing plastic onto surface of custard. Set aside.

Preheat oven to 375°. Unroll fila and lay flat; cover with plastic wrap to prevent drying. Brush bottom and sides of a 10 by 15 by 2-inch roasting pan with some of the ⅔ cup melted butter. Place one sheet of fila in pan, pressing edges to pan sides; brush sheet of fila with butter. Continue layering fila and brushing with butter until ⅔ of fila has been used.

Spread custard over fila in pan; layer on remaining fila sheets, brushing each with butter. Score top into 24 squares, cutting through 3 or 4 layers of fila. Bake until lightly browned (about 45 minutes). Place on a rack; let cool to room temperature. Meanwhile, prepare Cinnamon Syrup.

To serve, cut pastry into squares; drizzle each square with syrup. Makes 24 pieces.

Cinnamon Syrup. In a pan, combine ½ cup **sugar,** ⅓ cup **water,** 1 tablespoon **lemon juice,** and 1 **cinnamon stick** (about 3 inches long). Boil, stirring, until sugar is dissolved. Remove from heat; let cool.

Baklava

Perhaps the best-known fila dessert, *baklava* combines layers of pastry and lots of finely chopped walnuts, all bound with a honey syrup.

 4 cups finely chopped walnuts
 ⅔ cup sugar
 1½ teaspoons grated orange peel
 ½ teaspoon ground cinnamon
 1 cup (½ lb.) butter, melted
 1 package (1 lb.) fila (thawed if frozen)
 ¼ cup *each* sugar and water
 1½ cups honey
 1 tablespoon orange-flavored liqueur

Preheat oven to 300°. Combine walnuts, the ⅔ cup sugar, orange peel, and cinnamon; set aside. Brush bottom of a 9 by 13-inch baking pan with some of the butter. Unroll fila and lay flat; cover with plastic wrap to prevent drying. Brush one sheet of fila with butter; fold in half crosswise and place in pan. Repeat with 3 more sheets.

Sprinkle about ⅓ cup of the walnut mixture over dough. Brush one more sheet of fila with butter; fold in half and place over nut mixture. Continue layering fila and nut mixture until you have 12 nut layers; place 4 more sheets of fila, buttered and folded, atop last nut layer. (You'll have a few leftover sheets of fila.) Using a sharp knife, score top in a diamond pattern, making cuts 1½ to 2 inches apart. Bake until golden brown (about 1¼ hours).

Meanwhile, place the ¼ cup sugar and water in a pan. Bring to a boil, stirring until sugar is dissolved. Remove from heat. Stir in honey and liqueur; let cool. Pour syrup over hot pastry; let cool. Makes about 36 pieces.

Apple Strudel

The same flaky pastry that goes into Middle Eastern delicacies also wraps around fresh fruit, nuts, or sweet cheese fillings to make fine European strudel.

- 3 **large tart apples** (about 1½ lbs. *total*), peeled, cored, and thinly sliced
- 1 **tablespoon lemon juice**
- ¾ **cup sugar**
- ½ **teaspoon ground cinnamon**
- ⅓ **cup** *each* **raisins and finely chopped walnuts**
- 8 **sheets fila** (thawed if frozen)
- 6 **tablespoons butter,** melted

Preheat oven to 375°. In a large bowl, combine apples, lemon juice, ½ cup of the sugar, cinnamon, raisins, and walnuts. Set aside.

Unroll fila and lay flat; cover with plastic wrap to prevent drying. Brush one sheet of fila with some of the melted butter; top with one more sheet and brush with butter. Repeat layering and buttering with 2 more sheets of fila.

Sprinkle 2 tablespoons of the remaining sugar in a strip 1½ inches in from one long side of top sheet of fila, extending to about 1 inch of ends. Spoon half the apple mixture evenly atop sugar. Fold in ends of fila over filling; then fold side over filling and roll up jelly roll style. Carefully place roll, seam side down, on a lightly greased baking sheet. Brush all over with butter.

Repeat with remaining fila, butter, sugar, and apple mixture. Bake until lightly browned (about 20 minutes). To serve, slice with a serrated knife. Makes 2 rolls (8 to 10 servings *total*).

Cherry Strudel

Follow directions for **Apple Strudel,** but substitute this cherry filling for the apple mixture.

Spread 5 tablespoons slivered **almonds** in a shallow baking pan; toast in a 350° oven until lightly browned (about 5 minutes). Set aside.

In a bowl, stir together 2 cups pitted fresh **cherries** (or unsweetened frozen cherries, thawed and drained), ½ cup **sugar,** ⅓ cup **golden raisins,** 1 teaspoon grated **lemon peel,** and ¼ teaspoon **almond extract.** Butter, layer, fill, and roll fila as directed for **Apple Strudel,** using 3 sheets fila, 2 tablespoons sugar, and half the cherry mixture for each roll. For each roll, top cherry mixture with 2½ tablespoons of the toasted slivered almonds before rolling.

Almond Strudel

Follow directions for **Apple Strudel,** but substitute this almond filling for the apple mixture.

Spread ⅔ cup finely ground **almonds** in a shallow baking pan; toast in a 350° oven until lightly browned (about 5 minutes). Set aside.

In large bowl of an electric mixer, beat 2 **eggs** until thick and lemon colored; add ½ cup **sugar,** 1 tablespoon at a time, beating well after each addition. Fold in almonds, ½ teaspoon *each* grated **lemon peel** and **vanilla,** and, if desired, ¼ teaspoon **almond extract.** Butter, layer, fill, and roll fila as directed for **Apple Strudel,** but omit sugar. Use half the almond mixture for each roll. (If some of the filling leaks through fila during baking, cut off and discard before serving.)

Cheese Strudel

Follow directions for **Apple Strudel,** but substitute this cheese filling for the apple mixture.

In a bowl, stir together 2 tablespoons **currants** and 1 tablespoon **brandy;** set aside. In large bowl of an electric mixer, beat ½ pound (about 1 cup) **farmers cheese** or dry curd cottage cheese, 3 **egg yolks,** 1 small package (3 oz.) **cream cheese** (softened), and ½ cup **sugar** until smooth. Stir in currants, brandy, and 1 teaspoon grated **lemon peel.** Butter, layer, fill, and roll fila as directed for **Apple Strudel,** but omit sugar. Use half the cheese mixture for each roll.

Working with Fila

Always thaw frozen fila completely before using: let the unopened package stand overnight in the refrigerator. To make fresh or thawed frozen dough easier to handle, let stand at room temperature for 1 hour before shaping. If only part of a package is needed, wrap the rest airtight and refrigerate for up to 2 weeks; or freeze for up to 6 months.

Because fila is so thin, the sheets dry out quickly when exposed to air. To prevent drying, keep dough covered with plastic wrap as you work. If a sheet of dough has cracks around the edges, simply cut off the cracked portions and use the trimmed sheet. If the sheets tear when you fold or butter them, just overlap the edges.

Yeast Pastries

Neither bread nor pastry, but somewhere in between. That's one way to describe these tempting treats. Yeast-leavened doughs enriched with butter, eggs, and milk produce fine, flaky croissants and tender coffeecakes and sweet rolls—filled or glazed, formed into special shapes, and delightful to eat any time of day.

Filled Croissants

(Pictured on facing page)

The secret to achieving light, flaky croissants is in the folding and rolling process, in which thin sheets of butter are layered throughout the dough. It's best to keep the butter and dough cool while you work, so use a cool surface (such as marble or plastic laminate) if possible.

A few words about ingredients: For best flavor and texture, use butter, not margarine. You'll also get a better croissant if you use bread flour; it makes a stronger dough that holds up better during shaping and baking.

> 1 **package active dry yeast**
> ¼ **cup warm water (about 110°F)**
> ¾ **cup warm milk (about 110°F)**
> 1 **tablespoon sugar**
> ½ **teaspoon salt**
>   **About 2½ cups bread flour**
> 1 **cup (two ¼-lb. sticks) cold unsalted butter**
>   **Almond, Chocolate, Chocolate-Almond, or Fruit Filling (recipes follow)**
> 1 **egg yolk beaten with 1 tablespoon milk**

In large bowl of a heavy-duty mixer, dissolve yeast in warm water. Stir in milk, sugar, and salt. Gradually add 2⅓ cups of the flour and beat on high speed until dough is elastic and pulls away from sides of bowl in stretchy strands—about 5 minutes. (Or beat vigorously by hand for about 15 minutes.) Cover and let rise in a warm place until doubled (1 to 1½ hours). Then scrape dough onto a lightly floured baking sheet, cover with plastic wrap, and refrigerate until very cold (about 30 minutes).

Meanwhile, using a sharp knife, cut each stick of butter crosswise into very thin slices. Place on wax paper and refrigerate.

Sprinkle about 1 tablespoon of the remaining flour on a cool surface. Slide dough from baking sheet onto flour; roll out to a rectangle about ¼ inch thick. Arrange butter slices, slightly overlapping, in center of dough rectangle. Fold extending sides over butter; roll out again until rectangle is about ⅜ inch thick. If necessary, turn dough over occasionally and flour surface lightly to prevent sticking; use as little flour as possible. Fold dough into thirds again to make a squarish rectangle. Roll and fold dough again in the same way; then wrap folded dough in plastic wrap and refrigerate for 30 minutes.

Roll and fold chilled dough 2 more times, just as before; then wrap in plastic wrap and refrigerate for 15 to 30 minutes. Meanwhile, prepare filling of your choice.

Roll out dough to a rectangle about ⅛ inch thick. Cut into 16 triangles, each about 6 inches across the base and 8 inches tall. Place filling about 1 inch above base of each triangle. Roll triangles up from base to point and place, point down, on ungreased baking sheets; croissants should be about 1½ inches apart all around. Curve ends inward to form a crescent shape. Cover lightly and let rise in a warm place until very puffy (about 2 hours).

Preheat oven to 400°. Brush croissants lightly with egg yolk mixture. Bake until golden brown (20 to 25 minutes). Serve hot, or transfer to racks and let cool. Makes 16.

Almond Filling. In a blender or food processor, whirl ⅓ cup unblanched whole **almonds** until finely ground. Add ⅓ cup *each* **all-purpose flour** and **powdered sugar.** Then add ⅓ cup firm **unsalted butter** (cut into chunks) and ¼ teaspoon **almond extract;** whirl until combined. (Or work together almonds and remaining ingredients with a fork.)

Fill each croissant with 1 tablespoon filling rolled into a 3-inch-long log. After brushing croissants with egg yolk mixture, sprinkle with sliced **almonds.**

Chocolate Filling. Break each of 4 **semisweet chocolate bars** (about 1½ oz. *each*) into 12 small rectangles; fill each croissant with 3 rectangles, slightly overlapping.

Chocolate-Almond Filling. Prepare **Almond Filling,** but press 2 small rectangles **semisweet chocolate** (see **Chocolate Filling**) into each 3-inch log of filling.

Fruit Filling. Fill each croissant with 1 tablespoon **canned fruit pie filling,** such as apple, cherry, blueberry, or peach.

Chocolate-filled Croissants

1 On a cool surface, roll out dough to a rectangle. Arrange butter slices, lightly overlapping, in center third of rectangle; fold sides over butter.

2 Roll out folded dough to a rectangle, turning dough and sprinkling surface lightly with flour if necessary. Fold dough into thirds; then re-roll and fold again. Refrigerate.

3 Roll out dough to a rectangle about ⅛ inch thick. Cut into 16 triangles, each 6 inches across the base and 8 inches tall.

4 Place 3 rectangles of chocolate across each triangle, just above base. Roll triangles up from base to point and place on baking sheets; curve ends.

Buttery Almond Bear Claws

Rich, almondy bear claws are usually considered a bakery specialty. But with our easy refrigerator dough and streamlined technique, you'll make bear claws that rival the best you can buy.

  1 cup (½ lb.) butter or margarine
  1 package active dry yeast
  ¼ cup warm water (about 110°F)
  3 eggs
  ¼ cup sugar
  ½ teaspoon salt
  1 small can (5⅓ oz.) evaporated milk
    About 3⅓ cups all-purpose flour
    Almond Filling (recipe follows)
    About ¾ cup sliced almonds
    Sugar

Melt butter in a small pan, then let cool to 110°F. In a bowl, dissolve yeast in warm water. Separate eggs; place 2 of the whites in a bowl and set aside to use for filling. Cover and refrigerate remaining white. Stir egg yolks into yeast mixture along with the ¼ cup sugar, salt, milk, and cooled butter.

Place 3⅓ cups of the flour in a large bowl, pour in yeast mixture, and beat well. Cover and refrigerate for at least 1 day or up to 3 days. Prepare Almond Filling; refrigerate.

To shape bear claws, punch down dough and knead briefly on a well-floured board to release air. Roll out to a 13½ by 27-inch rectangle, using a ruler to straighten edges. Cut dough lengthwise into 3 strips, each 4½ inches wide. Divide filling into thirds; on a floured board, roll each portion into a 27-inch rope. Lay an almond rope in center of each dough strip; flatten rope slightly with your fingers.

Fold long sides of each strip over filling, then cut each filled strip into six 4½-inch-long sections. Arrange sections, seam side down, on greased baking sheets.

Using a floured sharp knife, make a row of cuts at ¾-inch intervals from end to end of each section; cut through to bottom of section and about halfway across it each time. Curve each section so cut pieces fan out to make "claws."

Lightly beat remaining egg white and brush over bear claws; top with almonds and sprinkle lightly with sugar. Let rise in a warm place, uncovered, until puffy (about 20 minutes).

Preheat oven to 375°. Bake bear claws until golden brown (about 15 minutes). Transfer to racks and let cool. Makes 18.

Almond Filling. Smoothly blend ½ cup (¼ lb.) **butter** or margarine (softened) with 1⅓ cups **powdered sugar.** Add ⅔ cup **all-purpose flour** and 1 can (8 oz.) **almond paste.** Stir until crumbly and evenly mixed; beat in 1 teaspoon grated **lemon peel** and 2 **egg whites.** Stir in ¾ cup finely chopped **almonds.** Cover; refrigerate until firm (several hours) or for up to 3 days.

Cherry-Almond Wreath

A new twist makes this breakfast wreath a colorful treat for holiday time.

  1 package active dry yeast
  ¼ cup warm water (about 110°F)
  ½ cup warm milk (about 110°F)
  3 tablespoons sugar
  1½ teaspoons salt
  ½ teaspoon ground cardamom
  1 teaspoon grated lemon peel
  2 eggs
  ¼ cup butter or margarine, softened
    About 3½ cups all-purpose flour
    Cherry-Almond Filling (recipe follows)
    Sugar Glaze (recipe follows)

In large bowl of an electric mixer, dissolve yeast in warm water. Stir in milk, sugar, salt, cardamom, lemon peel, eggs, and butter. Beat in 2 cups of the flour, a cup at a time. Then beat on medium speed for 3 minutes, scraping bowl frequently.

With a heavy-duty mixer or a wooden spoon, beat in enough of the remaining flour (about 1¼ cups) to make a soft dough. Turn out onto a floured board; knead until smooth (5 to 10 minutes), adding flour as needed to prevent sticking. Place dough in a greased bowl; turn to grease top. Cover and let rise in a warm place until doubled (about 1½ hours). Meanwhile, prepare filling; cover and refrigerate.

Punch down dough and knead briefly on a floured board to release air; then roll out to a 9 by 30-inch rectangle. Crumble filling and scatter it over dough to within 1 inch of edges. Starting with one long side, roll up dough tightly, jelly roll style. Moisten edge with water and pinch firmly to seal.

Using a floured sharp knife, cut roll in half lengthwise to make 2 ropes; carefully turn cut sides up. Loosely twist ropes around each other, keeping cut sides up. Carefully transfer to a greased and flour-dusted baking sheet and shape into a 10-

inch ring; pinch ends together firmly to seal. Let rise in a warm place, uncovered, until puffy (45 to 60 minutes).

Preheat oven to 375°. Bake wreath until lightly browned (about 20 minutes). Run wide spatulas under wreath to loosen; transfer to a rack. Prepare Sugar Glaze and drizzle over wreath while still warm. Makes 1 large wreath.

Cherry-Almond Filling. In large bowl of an electric mixer, beat ¼ cup **butter** or margarine (softened), ¼ cup **all-purpose flour,** and 2 tablespoons **sugar** until smooth. Stir in ⅔ cup finely chopped blanched **almonds,** ¼ cup *each* **red and green candied cherries,** ½ teaspoon grated **lemon peel,** and ¾ teaspoon **almond extract.**

Sugar Glaze. In a small bowl, blend ⅔ cup **powdered sugar,** 1½ teaspoons **lemon juice,** and 1 tablespoon **water** until smooth.

Coffeecake Braid

This coffeecake has a bakery-bought look that makes it perfect for a brunch buffet.

    1 **package active dry yeast**
   ¼ **cup warm water (about 110°F)**
   ¼ **cup warm milk (about 110°F)**
   ½ **teaspoon salt**
   ¼ **cup sugar**
   1 **egg**
   6 **tablespoons butter or margarine, softened**
2½ **to 3 cups all-purpose flour**
      Poppy Seed, Apricot, Apple, or Cheese Filling (recipes follow)
   1 **egg white beaten with 1 teaspoon water**
   2 **tablespoons sliced almonds**

In a large bowl of an electric mixer, dissolve yeast in warm water. Stir in milk, salt, sugar, egg, and butter. Gradually beat in about 2½ cups of the flour to make a soft dough.

Turn dough out onto a lightly floured board; knead until smooth and satiny (10 to 15 minutes), adding flour as needed to prevent sticking. Place dough in a greased bowl and turn to grease top. Cover and let rise in a warm place until doubled (1 to 1½ hours). Meanwhile, prepare filling of your choice.

Punch down dough; knead briefly on a lightly floured board to release air. Roll out to a 10 by 15-inch rectangle, using a ruler to straighten edges. Place on a lightly greased large baking sheet. Mark dough lengthwise into 3 sections. Spread filling over center section. Using a sharp knife, cut each of the 2 outer sections into 10 diagonal strips, cutting in almost as far as filling. Cross strips over filling—one from right side, then one from left, alternating until all strips are folded over filling. Tuck any excess dough at end beneath loaf.

Brush loaf with egg white mixture and sprinkle with almonds. Let rise in a warm place, uncovered, until almost doubled (about 30 minutes).

Preheat oven to 350°. Bake loaf until richly browned (25 to 30 minutes). Transfer to a rack and let cool. Makes 1 large loaf.

Poppy Seed Filling. In a blender or food processor, whirl ¾ cup *each* **poppy seeds** and blanched whole **almonds** until mixture has the consistency of cornmeal. Transfer mixture to a small pan and add ½ cup **sugar,** ⅓ cup **milk,** ¾ teaspoon grated **lemon peel,** 1 tablespoon **lemon juice,** and 3 tablespoons **butter** or margarine. Cook over low heat, stirring, until mixture boils and thickens (about 10 minutes). Remove from heat and let filling cool to room temperature.

Apricot Filling. In a pan, combine 1¼ cups **dried apricots** (cut up), 1 cup **water,** ⅓ cup **honey,** and ⅛ teaspoon **ground cinnamon.** Bring to a boil over medium-high heat; then reduce heat and simmer, uncovered, until apricots are tender and liquid is absorbed (10 to 15 minutes). Remove from heat and let filling cool to room temperature.

Apple Filling. In a 2-quart pan, combine 4 cups peeled, sliced tart **apples,** 1½ tablespoons **lemon juice,** and 2 teaspoons **water.** Bring to a boil over medium-high heat; reduce heat and simmer, uncovered, until apples are tender (about 7 minutes). Stir together ½ cup **sugar,** 2 tablespoons **all-purpose flour,** and ¼ teaspoon *each* **ground cinnamon** and **ground nutmeg;** stir into apples and cook, stirring, until thickened. Stir in ½ cup **raisins.** Remove from heat and let filling cool to room temperature.

To fill coffeecake, sprinkle ¼ cup firmly packed **brown sugar** over center section of dough; top evenly with apple filling. Cut side strips to within ½ inch of filling. Omit almonds.

Cheese Filling. In small bowl of an electric mixer, beat 1 large package (8 oz.) **cream cheese** (softened), 1 **egg yolk,** 6 tablespoons **sugar,** 1 teaspoon grated **lemon peel,** and ½ teaspoon **vanilla** until smooth and well combined. Stir in ½ cup **golden raisins.** Omit almonds. Dust finished pastry with **powdered sugar,** if desired.

Cream Puffs

1 Stir vigorously with a wooden spoon until flour-butter mixture forms a ball and leaves sides of pan. Remove from heat.

2 As you beat in each egg, mixture separates into slippery clumps, but smooths out again after egg is completely mixed in.

3 To form cream puffs, scoop batter up in one spoon; push it off onto baking sheet with another spoon. During baking, mounds puff up into crisp, golden, irregularly shaped shells.

4 After puffs have cooled, carefully cut top (upper third) from each puff and scoop out moist, doughy interior. Fill just before serving.

Pastries from Chou Paste

Tiny cream puffs, elegant éclairs, and a grand Paris Crown are all made from chou paste—a simple mixture of melted butter, flour, and eggs. Chou paste is leavened by steam: as it's heated in the oven, the liquid turns to steam and the batter swells, baking into a crisp, golden brown shell with a hollow interior. The puffy shells are perfect containers for almost any sweet filling; the most popular choices include pastry cream, sweetened whipped cream, and ice cream.

Cream Puffs

(Pictured on facing page and on front cover)

A perfectly made cream puff should have a hollow, moist interior and a crisp, irregularly shaped outer shell with a somewhat pebbly surface. Like popovers, these delicate puffs collapse if they're underbaked.

> Chou Paste (recipe follows)
> Uncooked Pastry Cream (recipe follows) or sweetened whipped cream
> Powdered sugar

Preheat oven to 425°. Prepare Chou Paste. To shape cream puffs, spoon batter into a pastry bag fitted with a large plain tip; or just scoop out batter with a spoon. Use about 2 tablespoons batter for each medium-size puff, about 1 tablespoon for each small puff. Space mounds of batter about 2 inches apart on greased baking sheets.

Bake in upper third of oven for 15 minutes. Reduce oven heat to 375°; cut a slash in the bottom of each puff, then continue to bake until puffs are firm, dry to the touch, and golden brown (about 10 more minutes). Transfer to racks and let cool completely. Use puffs as soon as they're cooled; or wrap airtight and let stand at room temperature for up to 24 hours. (Or wrap airtight and freeze for up to 1 month.)

To serve, prepare Uncooked Pastry Cream. Using a sharp knife, carefully cut the top third from each puff; scoop out and discard the moist, doughy interior. Just before serving, place pastry cream in a pastry bag fitted with a large plain tip

and pipe filling into puffs (or simply spoon filling into puffs). Replace tops and dust lightly with powdered sugar. Makes about 24 medium-size cream puffs, 36 to 48 small cream puffs.

Chou Paste. In a 3-quart pan, combine 1 cup **water,** ½ cup (¼ lb.) **butter** or margarine, ¼ teaspoon **salt,** and 1 teaspoon **sugar.** Bring to a boil over medium-high heat, stirring to melt butter. When butter is melted, remove pan from heat and add 1 cup **all-purpose flour** all at once. Beat with a wooden spoon until well blended.

Reduce heat to medium. Return pan to heat and stir vigorously with a wooden spoon until mixture forms a ball and leaves sides of pan. Remove pan from heat; let mixture cool for 5 minutes. Add 4 **eggs,** one at a time, beating until smooth after each addition. (Mixture will break apart into slippery clumps after each egg is added, but will return to a smooth paste after egg is completely mixed in by vigorous beating.)

Uncooked Pastry Cream. In small bowl of an electric mixer, beat 2 small packages (3 oz. *each*) **cream cheese** (softened) on high speed until smooth. Beating constantly, pour in 2 cups **whipping cream** in a steady stream. Mixture should have the consistency of stiffly whipped cream at all times; if it looks too soft, stop adding cream until it thickens. *Do not overbeat* after all cream has been added or mixture will separate.

Stir in 1 cup **powdered sugar,** 1 teaspoon *each* **vanilla** and grated **lemon peel,** and 2 teaspoons **lemon juice.** If made ahead, cover and refrigerate until next day. Makes about 5 cups.

Chestnut-filled Cream Puffs

You will need about 30 small cream puffs.

For the filling, combine 1 can (17 oz.) **sweetened chestnut purée** and 1 tablespoon *each* **dark rum** and **orange-flavored liqueur** in a large bowl. In the top of a double boiler over simmering water (or over lowest possible direct heat), melt 2 ounces **unsweetened chocolate,** stirring constantly. Stir melted chocolate into chestnut mixture.

In another bowl, beat 1 cup **whipping cream** until it holds stiff peaks; beat in 2 tablespoons **sugar** and 1 teaspoon **vanilla.** Fold into chestnut mixture. If made ahead, cover and refrigerate for up to 4 hours; let stand at room temperature until slightly softened before using.

To assemble, split puffs as directed for **Cream Puffs;** fill with chestnut mixture and replace tops. Dust lightly with **powdered sugar,** if desired. Makes about 30 puffs.

Gâteau St.-Honoré

Named after the patron saint of French bakers, *gâteau St.-Honoré* is one of the more elaborate classic desserts. Small cream puffs are anchored with caramelized sugar to the rim of a pastry round; the center is filled with custard.

> **Sweet Butter Pastry for an 11-inch tart (page 8)**
> **Custard Sauce (recipe follows)**
> 1⅓ cups whipping cream
> **About 16 small cream puffs (page 71)**
> **About ½ cup granulated sugar**
> 4 cups hulled strawberries
> 1 tablespoon kirsch (optional)
> **Powdered sugar**

Preheat oven to 300°. Press pastry evenly over bottom of a 9 or 10-inch spring-form pan. Bake until pale gold all over (about 35 minutes). Place on a rack and let cool; remove pan sides.

Prepare and cool Custard Sauce. Beat 1 cup of the cream until it holds stiff peaks. Transfer ⅔ cup of the whipped cream to a small bowl; fold in ⅓ of the Custard Sauce. Set aside to use for cream puff filling.

To make pastry filling, fold remaining Custard Sauce into remaining whipped cream. Refrigerate, stirring occasionally, until thickened (45 minutes to 1½ hours). Check often; filling must be soft enough to pour. If it becomes too firm, it will look lumpy.

While pastry filling chills, place cream puff filling in a pastry bag fitted with a narrow plain tip; pierce side of each cream puff with tip and pipe in filling. (Stir any leftover filling into pastry filling.) Refrigerate filled puffs.

Place ½ cup of the granulated sugar in an 8 to 10-inch frying pan. Cook over medium heat, shaking pan frequently, until sugar liquefies and turns amber. Keep pan over very low heat to keep sugar liquid (or reheat to thin, as needed).

Remove pastry round from pan bottom and transfer to a rimless platter. Dip bottom of one puff in caramel syrup; set at edge of pastry round. Repeat with remaining puffs, placing them snugly around edge of pastry. Spoon remaining caramel syrup carefully over puffs.

Spoon pastry filling onto pastry base. Cover and refrigerate until firm (about 1 hour) or until next day. Meanwhile, reserve a few strawberries for garnish; place remaining berries in a blender or food processor and whirl until puréed. Add kirsch, if desired, and granulated sugar to taste. If made ahead, cover and refrigerate until next day.

Beat remaining ⅓ cup cream until it holds stiff peaks; add powdered sugar to taste. Place whipped cream in a pastry bag fitted with a large rosette tip; pipe rosettes around base of pastry. Garnish with reserved strawberries. Cut into wedges; pass strawberry sauce at the table. Makes about 10 servings.

Custard Sauce. In the top of a double boiler, mix 1½ teaspoons **unflavored gelatin** with ¼ cup **sugar**. Stir in 1 cup **milk** and bring to scalding directly over medium heat. In a small bowl, beat 2 **egg yolks** until blended; stir in about ¼ cup of the hot milk mixture, then return to top of double boiler, stirring constantly.

Place top of double boiler over simmering water. Stir with a wire whisk until custard has thickened enough to thickly coat a metal spoon (10 to 15 minutes). Remove from heat. Stir in 1 tablespoon **kirsch** (optional) and ½ teaspoon **vanilla**. Stir over ice water to cool quickly.

If made ahead, cover and refrigerate until next day. To soften, place sauce directly over low heat and stir constantly with a wire whisk until smooth and pourable, but still thick. If sauce gets too hot, refrigerate briefly, stirring occasionally.

Éclairs

Éclairs are simple to make at home—they're just strips of chou paste, filled with custard and topped with a chocolate glaze.

> **Vanilla Pastry Cream (recipe follows)**
> ½ recipe Chou Paste (page 71)
> **Chocolate Glaze (recipe follows)**

Prepare Vanilla Pastry Cream; set aside. Preheat oven to 425°. Prepare Chou Paste. For each éclair, use about ¼ cup batter. Place mounds of batter 2 to 3 inches apart on greased baking sheets; using a small metal spatula, spread each mound into a strip 3½ inches long and 1 inch wide. (Or spoon batter into a pastry bag fitted with a large plain tip; pipe onto baking sheets in 1 by 3½-inch strips.) Bake and cool as for Cream Puffs (page 71).

Prepare Chocolate Glaze. Split cooled éclairs horizontally; fill with pastry cream and replace tops. Drizzle with glaze. Makes about 12.

Vanilla Pastry Cream. In a bowl, beat 6 **egg yolks** and ½ cup **sugar** until combined. Stir in 5 tablespoons **all-purpose flour.** Measure 2 cups **milk;** stir enough into yolk mixture to make a smooth paste, then scald remaining milk in a 3-quart pan over medium-high heat. Stir hot milk into yolk mixture; then return all to pan and cook over medium-low heat, stirring constantly, until mixture boils and thickens. Stir in 1 teaspoon **vanilla.** Remove from heat and stir until slightly cooled.

Transfer pastry cream to a bowl. Place 2 tablespoons **butter** or margarine on top and let melt over surface. Let cool completely; stir before using. If made ahead, cover and refrigerate until next day. Makes about 2½ cups.

Chocolate Glaze. Coarsely chop 6 ounces **semi-sweet chocolate;** place in a small pan and add 9 tablespoons **whipping cream.** Cook over medium-low heat, stirring constantly, until chocolate is melted and well blended with cream.

Paris Crown

This Parisian specialty is a wonderful treat to serve with afternoon tea or coffee.

 ½ **recipe Chou Paste (page 71)**
    Coffee Cream (recipe follows)
 1 **cup whipping cream**
 ½ **teaspoon vanilla**
    Powdered sugar

Preheat oven to 375°. Prepare Chou Paste and spoon into a pastry bag fitted with a large rosette or plain tip. Pipe batter onto a greased baking sheet, making a ring about 1½ inches thick and 8 inches in outside diameter.

Bake until golden brown (about 50 minutes). Slide onto a rack. While ring is still hot, slice off the top third horizontally and push cut-off portion aside slightly. Let cool completely. If made ahead, wrap airtight and let stand at room temperature for up to 24 hours; or freeze for up to 1 month.

Prepare Coffee Cream. Beat whipping cream until it holds soft peaks; add vanilla, then sweeten to taste with powdered sugar. Fold ½ cup of the whipped cream into Coffee Cream; cover and refrigerate, stirring occasionally, until slightly thickened (about 15 minutes).

To assemble, spoon Coffee Cream into base of cooled ring. Spoon whipped cream on top of Coffee Cream. Replace top; dust with powdered sugar, if desired. Makes 8 servings.

Coffee Cream. Prepare **Custard Sauce** as directed on facing page, but omit kirsch and stir 1 tablespoon **strong coffee** into cooled custard.

Prune Plum Puff

A hollow shell of chou paste forms the crust for this unusual tart; to make the filling, you arrange poached fresh prune plums atop orange-scented whipped cream.

 ½ **recipe Chou Paste (page 71)**
 ⅓ **cup granulated sugar**
 2 **tablespoons water**
 ¼ **teaspoon ground nutmeg**
 12 **large firm-ripe prune plums, halved and pitted**
 1 **cup whipping cream**
 2 **tablespoons powdered sugar**
 2 **tablespoons orange-flavored liqueur or ½ teaspoon grated orange peel**
 ½ **cup sour cream**

Preheat oven to 400°. Prepare Chou Paste; spoon into a greased 9-inch spring-form pan and spread over pan bottom and about 2 inches up sides. Bake until puffy and golden brown (about 40 minutes). Turn off oven. Pierce crust with a wooden pick in 10 to 12 places and leave in closed oven for about 10 minutes to dry. Remove pan from oven and place on a rack; let puff cool completely, then remove pan sides.

If made ahead, cover loosely with foil and let stand at room temperature until next day. Re-crisp crust before serving: place on a baking sheet and heat, uncovered, in a 400° oven for 10 minutes. Place on a rack and let cool.

In a 10 to 12-inch frying pan, combine granulated sugar, water, and nutmeg; stir over low heat until sugar is dissolved. Set plums, cut side down, in pan; cover and simmer until tender when pierced (5 to 8 minutes). Let cool in syrup; then refrigerate, covered, until cold (about 30 minutes) or for up to 4 hours.

Beat whipping cream until it holds stiff peaks. Stir powdered sugar and liqueur into sour cream; fold into whipped cream. If made ahead, cover and refrigerate for up to 4 hours.

Spoon cream mixture into crust. Arrange plums on top, cut side down; drizzle with any unabsorbed syrup. Cut into wedges. Makes 6 to 8 servings.

Puff Pastry Specialties

By far the most elegant member of the pastry family, puff pastry is also the most difficult and time-consuming to prepare. For this reason, we recommend using purchased frozen puff pastry sheets or patty shells. Starting with ready-made pastry, you can build dazzling desserts in a fraction of the time that you'd need to make just the pastry from scratch. You need only prepare the topping or filling, then shape and bake. Choose spectacular napoleons or glorious tarts; or try the simple, elegant pastry "cookies" called palm leaves (*palmiers*). All are excellent choices when time is short and the occasion calls for a special dessert.

Chocolate-filled Pastry Horns

(Pictured on facing page)

Puff pastry horns filled with chocolate cream are just right for dessert after a light meal. You'll need cone-shaped metal molds to shape the horns; look for them in cookware shops.

- 1 sheet (half of a 17¼-oz. package) frozen puff pastry
- ½ cup sifted powdered sugar
- ¼ cup sifted unsweetened cocoa
- 2 cups whipping cream
- 2 bars (about 2 oz. *each*) solid milk chocolate, ¾ to 1 inch thick (at room temperature)

Thaw pastry at room temperature for 20 minutes.

Preheat oven to 450°. Unfold pastry. On a lightly floured board, roll out pastry to a 10 by 17-inch rectangle; cut into ten 1-inch-wide strips with a sharp knife. Wrap each strip around a 4½ by 1¾-inch metal cone. Start at tapered end, pinching pastry together to seal; then wrap strip around cone, turning cone with one hand and wrapping strip with the other. At each turn, overlap pastry by ¼ inch. When you reach large end of cone, moisten end of strip and gently blend into pastry beneath, using your fingertip.

Place cones on their sides on ungreased baking sheets. Bake until pastry is lightly browned (15 to 20 minutes). Transfer to a rack and let cool; carefully twist out metal cones.

While pastry horns cool, stir together sugar and cocoa and set aside. Whip cream until it holds soft peaks; then add cocoa mixture, 1 tablespoon at a time, and continue to beat until cream is stiff but still smooth. Spoon into a pastry bag fitted with a large plain or rosette tip; pipe into cooled pastry horns. If made ahead, cover and refrigerate for up to 4 hours.

Shave chocolate into curls (see photo 4 on the facing page and "Making Chocolate Curls" on page 40). Garnish horns with curls and grated chocolate, if desired. Makes 10.

Ground Almond Tart

Lemon-scented almond filling bakes between layers of puff pastry for this ethereal creation.

- 1 cup blanched almonds
- ½ cup granulated sugar
- 3 tablespoons butter, softened
- ¼ teaspoon almond extract
- 1 teaspoon grated lemon peel
- 2 eggs
- 1 package (10 oz.) frozen patty shells, thawed
- 3 tablespoons powdered sugar

Whirl almonds in a blender or food processor until finely ground. Place in large bowl of an electric mixer; add granulated sugar, butter, almond extract, lemon peel, 1 whole egg, and 1 egg yolk (reserve remaining egg white). Beat until smooth and creamy. Set aside.

Preheat oven to 450°. On a lightly floured board, arrange 2 patty shells with edges touching. Cut a third shell in half; arrange halves, cut sides facing out, next to the 2 whole shells to form a rough circle. Pinch edges of shells together, then roll out to a 10-inch circle. Repeat with remaining 3 shells to form a second circle.

Place one pastry circle on an ungreased baking sheet; spread with almond filling to within 1 inch of edges. Top with second circle. Press edges with a fork to seal. Decoratively slash top with a sharp knife. Lightly beat reserved egg white and brush over top, then evenly sift powdered sugar over top. Bake for 10 minutes. Reduce oven heat to 400° and continue to bake until well browned (about 10 more minutes). Serve at room temperature. Makes 8 servings.

Chocolate-filled Pastry Horns

 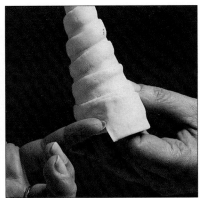  

Wrap pastry strip around metal cone. Start at tip, pinching pastry to seal; wrap up to wide end, overlapping pastry ¼ inch at each turn.

2 To prevent strip from unwrapping during baking, moisten end of strip with water and gently blend it and cut edges into pastry beneath, using fingertip or fingernail.

3 Whip cream until it holds soft peaks. Beating constantly, gradually add sugar-cocoa mixture, a tablespoon at a time. Continue to beat just until cream filling is stiff but still smooth.

4 To make chocolate curls, start with room-temperature chocolate. Press blade of vegetable peeler down into chocolate and draw it across surface.

Napoleons

(Pictured on page 62)

Strips of puff pastry are first baked blind, then layered with rich pastry cream for this French specialty. Be sure to prick the pastry strips thoroughly before baking, so they'll stay flat enough to hold the filling in place.

  1 envelope unflavored gelatin
  3 tablespoons cold water
    Double recipe French Pastry Cream (page 42)
  1 package (17¼ oz.) frozen puff pastry
  2 cups sifted powdered sugar
    About 3 tablespoons warm water
  ½ cup semisweet chocolate chips
  2 teaspoons light corn syrup

Sprinkle gelatin over the 3 tablespoons cold water; set aside to soften. Prepare French Pastry Cream. After stirring in vanilla, stir in gelatin mixture until dissolved. Cover and refrigerate until firm (about 6 hours) or until next day.

Thaw pastry at room temperature for 20 minutes. Preheat oven to 400°. Unfold one sheet of pastry; on a lightly floured board, roll out to a 10 by 18-inch rectangle. Using a sharp knife, cut crosswise into six 3 by 10-inch rectangles. Prick rectangles all over with a fork, pricking all the way through dough; then place on ungreased baking sheets, spacing about 1 inch apart. Repeat with remaining sheet of pastry.

Bake until light golden (10 to 12 minutes); transfer to racks and let cool. Cut each cooled rectangle in half crosswise.

Stir together sugar and 2 tablespoons of the warm water until smooth and easy to spread; set aside. Place chocolate chips, corn syrup, and 2 teaspoons of the warm water in a small pan; cook over low heat, stirring, just until chocolate is melted. Mixture should drizzle easily; if necessary, stir in up to 2 more teaspoons warm water.

Hold one pastry rectangle in your hand, flat side up; spread thinly with white icing. Immediately drizzle with chocolate mixture, making 3 parallel lengthwise lines. Then lightly drag a wooden skewer across iced pastry several times, at right angles to chocolate lines; drag first in one direction, then in the other, to create a design (see photo on page 62). Repeat with 7 more pastry rectangles. Place on racks and let stand until icing is set. (At this point, you may cover iced and plain pastry loosely with foil and let stand at room temperature until next day.)

Spread about ⅓ cup of the pastry cream on each of 16 plain rectangles. Stack in groups of 2, with cream sides up; top each stack with an iced rectangle. If made ahead, cover lightly and refrigerate for up to 6 hours. Makes 8.

Free-form Fruit Pastry

Packaged puff pastry streamlines the preparation of this professional-looking pastry. Bake a crisp, flaky raft topped with cheese or almond filling, then add your choice of fruit.

  1 sheet (half of a 17¼-oz. package) frozen
    puff pastry
    Cheese or Almond Filling (recipes follow)
  ⅓ cup red currant jelly or orange marmalade
    About 2 cups halved strawberries, sliced
    apricots, or sliced peaches (or 1 cup *each*
    of 2 different fruits)

Thaw pastry at room temperature for 20 minutes. Meanwhile, prepare your choice of filling.

Preheat oven to 425°. Place pastry on an ungreased 12 by 15-inch baking sheet and unfold. Spread filling down length of pastry, to about 1½ inches from both long sides; then fold sides of pastry over to cover edges of filling.

Bake until browned (12 to 15 minutes). Place baking sheet on a rack; let pastry cool completely. (At this point, you may cover loosely with foil and let cooled pastry stand at room temperature for up to 4 hours.)

Up to 1 hour before serving, melt jelly or marmalade in a small pan over low heat (use jelly with berries, marmalade with apricots or peaches). Lightly brush filling with some of the jelly. Arrange fruit over filling, overlapping pieces slightly. Brush with remaining jelly.

To serve, cut pastry into slices with a sharp knife. Makes 8 to 10 servings.

Cheese Filling. In small bowl of an electric mixer, beat 1 large package (8 oz.) **cream cheese** (softened), ⅓ cup **sugar**, 2 tablespoons **all-purpose flour**, 1 teaspoon **vanilla**, and ½ teaspoon grated **lemon peel** until smooth.

Almond Filling. In small bowl of an electric mixer, beat ¼ cup **butter** or margarine until creamy. Gradually add 1 package (7 oz.) **almond paste**, 1 **egg white**, and ½ teaspoon grated **lemon peel**; beat until smooth and well blended.

Hot Apple Tarts

Sliced fresh apples, pears, or apricots bake on individual rounds of puff pastry for a dessert with a charming, homey look.

The patty shells used for these tarts are sold in 10-ounce packages, each containing six shells. You need only four shells for this recipe; keep the leftover shells in the freezer for another use. (Or just multiply the amounts below by 1½ and make six tarts.)

> 4 **frozen patty shells, thawed**
> 2 **medium-size Golden Delicious apples**
> **About 2 tablespoons sugar**
> **About 3 tablespoons apple jelly or red currant jelly**
> **Whipping cream**
> **Applesauce (optional)**

Preheat oven to 400°. Place patty shells 2 to 3 inches apart on an ungreased baking sheet. Using your fingers, evenly press each shell to make a 5 to 6-inch circle.

Peel, core, and thinly slice apples; arrange slices in a circular pattern atop each pastry circle, overlapping them slightly. Sprinkle evenly with sugar.

Bake until crust is golden brown (20 to 25 minutes). About 2 minutes before the end of baking time, place about 2 teaspoons of the jelly in center of each tart; as soon as you remove baked tarts from oven, brush melted jelly evenly over surface. Serve hot.

At the table, offer whipping cream and, if desired, applesauce to spoon over individual servings. Makes 4.

Hot Pear Tarts

Follow directions for **Hot Apple Tarts,** but substitute 2 medium-size firm-ripe **pears** (such as Bartlett, Anjou, or Bosc) for apples. Omit applesauce.

Hot Apricot Tarts

Follow directions for **Hot Apple Tarts,** but omit apples. Instead, use 12 fresh **apricots,** peeled (if desired) and halved (use 6 halves for each tart). Sprinkle tarts with a mixture of 2 tablespoons **sugar** and ⅛ teaspoon **ground nutmeg.** Substitute **apricot jam** for apple jelly. If desired, substitute **sour cream** for whipping cream. Omit applesauce.

Puff Pastry Treats

Some of the most celebrated puff pastry classics are also among the simplest—just sugared pastry, cut and folded or twisted into various shapes. For Palm Leaves (*palmiers*), you roll and fold the pastry in sugar, then cut it into many-layered slices; for Cinnamon Twists, strips of pastry are rolled in cinnamon sugar, then twisted to form sweet, spiced spirals. Both are crunchy, cookie-like treats that make a perfect accompaniment for simple desserts such as ice cream or fresh fruit.

Palm Leaves. Thaw 1 sheet (half of a 17¼-oz. package) **frozen puff pastry** at room temperature for 20 minutes.

Sprinkle 2 tablespoons **sugar** on a board or pastry marble. Unfold pastry, place on sugar, and roll out to a 9 by 12-inch rectangle. Sprinkle evenly with 2 more tablespoons **sugar.** Fold each short side halfway to center; then fold in again, so folds meet in center. Then fold pastry in half to make a compact 6-layer roll. Cover with plastic wrap; refrigerate for at least 30 minutes or up to 1 hour. (Don't refrigerate for over 1 hour or sugar will begin to dissolve.)

Preheat oven to 400°. Cut pastry crosswise into ⅜-inch-thick slices; place 1½ inches apart on ungreased baking sheets. Bake for 10 minutes. Turn pastries over; continue to bake until evenly browned (about 5 more minutes). Transfer to racks and let cool. Makes about 30.

Cinnamon Twists. Thaw 1 sheet (half of a 17¼-oz. package) **frozen puff pastry** at room temperature for 20 minutes.

Preheat oven to 400°. In a small bowl, combine ½ teaspoon **ground cinnamon** and ¼ cup **sugar;** sprinkle half the mixture on a board or pastry marble. Place pastry on sugar mixture; roll out to a 10 by 12-inch rectangle. Evenly sprinkle with remaining sugar mixture. Cut pastry crosswise into ½-inch strips; then cut each strip in half crosswise. Hold ends of each strip and twist in opposite directions. Place twists slightly apart on ungreased baking sheets.

Bake until lightly browned (about 10 minutes). Transfer to racks and let cool. Makes 48.

Savory Pies & Pastries

Savory pastries, like their sweet counterparts, offer a dazzling diversity of taste and an intriguing history. From the homiest meat pie to the fragile elegance of a shattery puff pastry *vol-au-vent*, these creations have origins we can trace back to medieval times—or even earlier. "Four-and-twenty blackbirds, baked in a pie," celebrated in the nursery rhyme, whimsically describes a popular style of cooking of a much earlier day. The better-mannered descendants of that "dainty dish"—chicken breasts baked in tidy individual packets—can still be counted on to make fare fit for a king.

Pastry wrappings. When you enclose a substantial quantity of meat or fish in flaky pastry or puff pastry for a dinner entrée, you're guaranteed a dramatic and impressive presentation. Think of *pâté en croûte* on a summer's eve, or creamy-sauced veal chops nestled beneath a golden dome of puff pastry for an autumn dinner party.

Quiches and other custardy tarts also play a delicious part in both grand occasions and everyday meals. Savory pies such as Leek & Ham Quiche can be offered at a company brunch or a family supper—or even carried on a picnic to be served cold.

Handsome Veal & Ham Pâté en Croûte (recipe on page 80) makes an elegant cold entrée.

For more down-to-earth family food, bake beef, sausage, or chicken in a pie to make a wholesome dish such as Beef & Spinach Supper Pie. Accompanied with a green salad, such fare makes a meal that's both satisfying and out of the ordinary.

Fila pastries. Another member of the international pastry family is tissue-thin fila, a favorite in Greece and around the Mediterranean coast. Its crisp flakiness is as tempting a complement to the savory herbs and mixed greens in *spanakopita* (page 85) as it is to the honeyed nuts and spices in *baklava* (page 64). Working with this delicate-looking pastry is simpler than you might expect, and the results are always spectacular.

Party-time pastries. Warm, crisp pastries are always popular party food. You can make them with a variety of pastry wrappings or crusts—fila, convenient packaged puff pastry, or your own irresistible flaky butter pastry.

For gatherings large or small, bake Greek-style spicy lamb logs and feta cheese triangles, chicken or mushroom-filled open tarts in the French manner, or savory puff pastry twists layered with Swiss cheese. All these enticing morsels offer a big advantage for busy hostesses—they can be prepared ahead, then either baked or reheated later.

Pastry-wrapped Meats, Poultry & Fish

For guaranteed dining elegance, present a main dish enclosed in a flaky short crust or puff pastry.

Salmon Wellingtons

These salmon fillets are wrapped in puff pastry.

> 2 cups water
> 1 cup dry white wine
> 1 small carrot, thinly sliced
> 1 small onion, thinly sliced
> 1 bay leaf
> 10 whole black peppercorns
> 4 whole allspice
> ½ teaspoon *each* salt and thyme leaves
> 3 parsley sprigs
> 1½ pounds salmon fillet, about 1 inch thick
>   Mushroom Filling (recipe follows)
> 1 package (10 oz.) frozen patty shells, thawed
>   Lemon Sauce (recipe follows)

In a wide frying pan, combine water, wine, carrot, onion, bay leaf, peppercorns, allspice, salt, thyme, and parsley. Bring to a boil over high heat; reduce heat and simmer, uncovered, for 15 minutes.

Cut salmon into 6 pieces, each about 3 inches square. Place in pan, skin side down. Cover and simmer just until salmon is almost opaque throughout (7 to 10 minutes). Lift salmon from pan; discard skin. Let cool, then cover and refrigerate. Reserve poaching liquid for sauce.

Prepare Mushroom Filling. For each piece of salmon, roll out one patty shell on a floured board to an 8-inch circle. Put 1 tablespoon filling in center; top with salmon. Fold pastry over salmon, lapping edges at center. Place pastries, folded side down, on an ungreased rimmed baking sheet. Cover and refrigerate for up to 24 hours.

Preheat oven to 425°. Bake pastries on lowest rack of oven for 10 minutes. Meanwhile, prepare sauce. Move pastries to highest oven rack; continue to bake until golden brown (8 to 10 more minutes). Serve with sauce. Makes 6 servings.

Mushroom Filling. Melt 1 tablespoon **butter** or margarine in a medium-size frying pan over medium heat. Add ½ pound **mushrooms,** thinly sliced, and 2 **green onions** (including tops), thinly sliced. Cook, stirring, until liquid has evaporated (5 to 10 minutes). Let cool. Cover and refrigerate.

Lemon Sauce. Strain **salmon poaching liquid,** discarding vegetables and seasonings. Boil liquid over high heat, uncovered, until reduced to 1½ cups (or add water to make 1½ cups). Combine 1 tablespoon *each* **cornstarch** and **water;** stir into pan and cook, stirring, until sauce boils and thickens.

Beat 3 **egg yolks** with 2 to 3 tablespoons **lemon juice.** Stir some of the hot sauce into egg yolk mixture, then return all to pan. Cook over very low heat, stirring, just until thickened.

Veal & Ham Pâté en Croûte

(Pictured on page 78)

Pâté en croûte—ribbons of chicken and ham dotted with pistachios and surrounded by a flaky golden pastry—makes a splendid cold entrée.

> 1 pound boneless cooked ham
> 1 whole chicken breast (about 1 lb.), skinned, boned, and split
> ¼ cup brandy
>   Pâté Pastry (recipe follows)
> 2 tablespoons butter or margarine
> 1 shallot, finely chopped (about 2 tablespoons)
> 1 clove garlic, minced or pressed
> ¼ teaspoon *each* ground cloves, white pepper, and thyme leaves
> 2 eggs
> ⅓ cup whipping cream
> ½ teaspoon salt
> 1 pound ground veal or ground turkey
> ¼ cup pistachios

Cut half the ham into ½-inch-thick slices; cut slices into long, ½-inch-wide strips. Cut chicken into long, ½-inch-wide strips. Place chicken and ham strips in a bowl; pour brandy over them. Set aside. Prepare pastry and set aside. Grind remaining ham, using a food processor or a food chopper fitted with a medium blade; set aside.

Melt butter in a small frying pan over medium heat. Add shallot and cook, stirring occasionally, until soft and golden. Mix in garlic, cloves, pepper, and thyme; remove from heat.

Beat eggs with ¼ cup of the cream. Blend in salt, shallot mixture, ground ham, veal, and pistachios. Lift chicken and ham strips from brandy and set aside; blend brandy into meat mixture.

Preheat oven to 450°. On a floured board, roll out ¾ of the pastry to a 12 by 18-inch rectangle; cut lengthwise into three 4 by 18-inch strips. Press one strip over bottom of a 3 by 3 by 10-inch *pâté en croûte* mold with a removable bottom, extending strip up over ends of mold. Cover sides of mold with remaining strips, trimming ends to fit and letting sides extend over rim of mold. Moisten edges of pastry and press together to seal, lining mold completely. Pastry should extend about 1 inch beyond pan rim on all sides.

If you don't have a *pâté en croûte* mold, use a 4½ by 8½-inch loaf pan. Line pan with heavy-duty foil, folding about 2 inches of foil over pan rim on all sides. Grease foil and dust lightly with flour, then line pan with pastry strips.

Pat ⅓ of the meat mixture into mold. Top with half the chicken and ham strips, arranging them parallel to sides of mold and alternating meats to achieve a striped effect. Cover with half the remaining meat mixture; add remaining chicken and ham. Cover chicken and ham strips with remaining meat mixture.

Roll out remaining pastry to a 4 by 12-inch rectangle. Place over meat mixture. Trim edges and seal; then finish with a decorative edge (see page 13). If you wish, roll out pastry trimmings and cut into small decorative shapes; arrange over top of pastry. Cut a ½-inch-diameter hole in center of pastry to allow steam to escape during baking. Roll a small piece of foil into a cone; insert into hole. Brush pastry with remaining cream. Set mold in a shallow baking pan to catch drips.

Bake pâté for 15 minutes. Reduce oven heat to 350° and continue to bake until pastry is well browned and juices run clear when a knife is inserted in center (about 1¼ more hours).

Place mold on a rack and let pâté cool for 30 minutes. Carefully remove sides of mold. (Or lift pâté from loaf pan; peel off foil.) Let pâté cool for 30 more minutes, then slice. If made ahead, cover and refrigerate for up to 2 days; let stand at room temperature for 30 minutes before slicing. Makes 8 servings.

Pâté Pastry. In a large bowl, stir together 2¼ cups **all-purpose flour** and ½ teaspoon **salt.**

Cut ⅔ cup firm **butter** or margarine into pieces; mash 3 **hard-cooked egg yolks.** Add butter and egg yolks to flour mixture. Stir to coat, then cut into flour mixture with a pastry blender or 2 knives until fine particles form. Add 1 **egg** and mix until blended. Work dough with your hands until smooth; shape into a ball.

Golden-domed Tarragon Veal Chops

A crisp topping of puff pastry blankets succulent chops in a creamy sauce. Tiny new potatoes and asparagus are good accompaniments for this pastry-wrapped entrée.

> 6 **to 8 veal loin chops,** *each* **about ¾ inch thick (2½ to 3 lbs.** *total***)**
> **Salt, white pepper, and all-purpose flour**
> ¼ **cup butter or margarine**
> 1 **tablespoon salad oil**
> 1 **cup julienne strips cooked ham (about ½ by 2 inches)**
> ¾ **pound mushrooms, cut into quarters**
> ¼ **cup finely chopped parsley**
> ¾ **teaspoon dry tarragon**
> ⅓ **cup dry vermouth**
> 1 **tablespoon lemon juice**
> ¾ **cup whipping cream**
> 1 **sheet (half of a 17¼-oz. package) frozen puff pastry, thawed**
> 1 **egg yolk beaten with 1 teaspoon water**

Sprinkle chops with salt and pepper; dust with flour. Heat butter and oil in a 12 to 14-inch frying pan over medium-high heat until foamy; add chops. Cook until well browned on one side. Turn chops over, then arrange ham and mushrooms around them. Cook until chops are browned on other side; reduce heat to low. Sprinkle chops with parsley and tarragon, then add vermouth and lemon juice. Cover and simmer over low heat until chops are just tender (15 to 20 minutes).

Transfer chops, ham, and mushrooms to a shallow oval baking dish (about 8 by 12 inches). Add cream to pan; cook over high heat, stirring often, until sauce is slightly thickened and reduced by about half. Pour sauce over chops. Cover and refrigerate until cold or for up to 24 hours.

Roll out pastry slightly, then trim to make about 1 inch larger than baking dish on all sides. Moisten edges of pastry with some of the egg yolk mixture. Place pastry, egg side up, over dish; turn edges under so egg is against dish. Seal by pressing lightly with a fork. Refrigerate for at least 30 minutes or for up to 3 hours.

Preheat oven to 425°. Brush pastry with remaining egg yolk mixture. Bake until crust is very well browned (20 to 25 minutes). To serve, lift pieces of pastry onto warm plates, then place 1 or 2 chops on each. Spoon sauce, mushrooms, and ham over all. Makes 4 to 6 servings.

Tarts & Quiches

It all began with Quiche Lorraine. That classic savory custard proved so popular that variations on the theme were inevitable.

Mussel Tart Beausejour

(Pictured on facing page)

There's a generous quantity of succulent mussels in this butter-crusted main dish pie.

    2 pounds mussels
    1 cup dry white wine or water
       Golden Pastry (recipe follows)
    2 tablespoons butter or margarine
    2 shallots, finely chopped (about ¼ cup *total*)
    1 cup (4 oz.) shredded Gruyère or Swiss cheese
    ¼ cup finely chopped parsley
    4 eggs
    1 cup half-and-half (light cream)
    1 teaspoon Dijon mustard
    ½ teaspoon salt
    ¼ teaspoon *each* paprika and ground nutmeg
    ⅛ teaspoon white pepper

Sort mussels, discarding any with open shells that do not close when covered with water. Using a stiff brush, scrub shells well under running water. Pull out or cut off each mussel's tough brown hairlike "beard."

Place mussels in a 5 to 6-quart pan; add wine. Cover and boil gently over medium heat just until mussels open (about 5 minutes). Lift out mussels, discarding any with unopened shells; let cool.

Prepare pastry. Preheat oven to 425°. On a floured board, roll out pastry and line a 10-inch quiche dish or pie pan as directed on page 12; trim pastry even with rim of dish, or fold overhang under itself and finish with one of the decorative edges described on page 13. Partially bake pastry shell as directed on page 29, then let cool. Reduce oven heat to 350°.

Remove mussels from shells; set aside. Melt butter in a small frying pan over medium heat. Add shallots and cook, stirring often, until soft and golden. Spoon cheese into pastry shell; top with mussels, shallots, and 3 tablespoons of the parsley.

In a bowl, beat eggs, half-and-half, mustard, salt, paprika, nutmeg, and pepper until well combined. Pour over mussel mixture. Bake until a knife inserted in center comes out clean (35 to 40 minutes). Let stand for 10 minutes before cutting. Sprinkle with remaining 1 tablespoon parsley. Makes 6 servings.

Golden Pastry. In a bowl, mix 1½ cups **all-purpose flour** and ¼ teaspoon **salt**. Cut ⅓ cup firm **butter** or margarine into pieces. Add to flour mixture with ¼ cup **solid vegetable shortening;** cut into flour mixture with a pastry blender or 2 knives until fine particles form. Add 1 **egg,** lightly beaten. Stir with a fork until dough clings together. With your hands, gather dough into a ball.

Alsatian Onion Tart

Bits of bacon and an abundance of slowly cooked onions flavor this savory custard tart.

       Golden Pastry (recipe above)
    3 large onions (about 1½ lbs. *total*)
    ¼ cup butter or margarine
    4 thick slices bacon, cut into ½ by 1-inch strips
    3 eggs
    ½ cup whipping cream
    ½ teaspoon salt
    ⅛ teaspoon ground nutmeg

Prepare pastry. Preheat oven to 425°. Following directions on page 12, roll out pastry and line an 11-inch tart pan with a removable bottom, a 10-inch quiche dish, or a 10-inch pie pan. (If using a tart pan or quiche dish, trim pastry even with pan rim.) Partially bake crust as directed on page 29; let cool. Reduce oven heat to 350°.

Cut off ends of onions. Cut each onion in half lengthwise, then thinly slice each half lengthwise so it falls into slivers. Melt butter in a wide frying pan over medium heat. Add onions and cook, stirring often, until soft and golden (15 to 20 minutes). Meanwhile, cook bacon in a medium-size frying pan over medium heat until lightly browned; lift out and drain on paper towels. Mix bacon lightly with onions, then spread mixture evenly in pastry shell.

In a bowl, beat eggs, cream, salt, and nutmeg until well combined. Pour over onion mixture. Bake until lightly browned (30 to 35 minutes). Let stand for 10 minutes before removing pan sides and cutting. Makes 6 servings.

Mussel Tart Beausejour

1 Sort mussels and scrub shells well with a stiff brush. Then pull out or cut off tough brown hairlike "beard."

2 Steam mussels in white wine or water, boiling gently just until shells pop open to reveal the mollusks inside. Discard any mussels with unopened shells.

3 When mussels are cool enough to handle, remove from shells (you should have about 2 cups). Cooked mussels can be covered and refrigerated for up to a day.

4 Beat eggs with half-and-half, mustard, and seasonings. Pour over shallots, mussels, and shredded cheese in partially baked pastry shell.

Leek & Ham Quiche

Try this savory quiche for a wintertime brunch or supper. When spring asparagus comes into season, bake the shrimp version.

With either quiche, serve your favorite green salad or a platter of marinated vegetables. Fruit makes a good dessert; try fresh strawberries or papaya with a squeeze of lime.

Flaky Butter Pastry for a single-crust 9-inch pie (page 7)
2   **leeks (about 1 lb.** *total***)**
2   **tablespoons butter or margarine**
1½ **cups (6 oz.) shredded Swiss cheese**
1   **cup finely diced cooked ham**
4   **eggs**
1   **cup half-and-half (light cream)**
¼   **teaspoon** *each* **salt and dry mustard**
    Pinch *each* **of ground nutmeg and white pepper**

Preheat oven to 425°. Roll out pastry and line a 1½-inch-deep pie pan as directed on page 12, then partially bake as directed on page 29. Place on a rack. Reduce oven heat to 350°.

Trim and discard ends and tops from leeks, leaving about 1½ inches of dark green leaves. Discard tough outer leaves. Split leeks lengthwise; rinse well, then thinly slice crosswise. Melt butter in a medium-size frying pan over medium heat. Add leeks and cook, stirring often, until bright green and tender-crisp to bite (3 to 5 minutes).

Sprinkle ¾ cup of the cheese into pastry shell; evenly distribute leeks and ham over cheese. In a bowl, beat eggs, half-and-half, salt, mustard, nutmeg, and pepper until blended. Pour over leek mixture. Sprinkle with remaining ¾ cup cheese.

Bake until top is golden brown and a knife inserted in center comes out clean (40 to 45 minutes). Let stand for 10 minutes before cutting. Makes 6 servings.

Shrimp & Asparagus Quiche

Follow directions for **Leek & Ham Quiche,** but omit leeks, butter, and ham.

Use asparagus in place of leeks: snap off and discard tough ends from ¾ pound **asparagus;** cut off tips, then cut stalks into ½-inch lengths. Add stalks to **boiling salted water** in a 2-quart pan over high heat; when boil resumes, add tips. Cook just until asparagus is bright green and tender-crisp to bite (2 to 3 minutes). Drain well; pat dry with paper towels.

Use ½ pound **small cooked shrimp** in place of ham. Add ½ teaspoon grated **lemon peel** and 1 tablespoon **lemon juice** to egg mixture.

Almond-crusted Watercress Tarts

Bake these suave individual tarts to serve as a first course—or as a picnic entrée, accompanied with thinly sliced cold meats such as ham and turkey. They're delicious served either hot from the oven or at room temperature.

We suggest making the tart pastry with almonds, but you might also use pecans, walnuts, or hazelnuts. Any one makes a nutty-tasting crust that nicely complements the watercress filling.

Nutty Short Pastry for a single-crust 9-inch pie (page 7), made with almonds
1   **cup (4 oz.) shredded Gruyère or Swiss cheese**
2   **tablespoons butter or margarine**
¼   **teaspoon dry tarragon**
2   **cups lightly packed watercress sprigs**
3   **eggs**
½   **cup half-and-half (light cream)**
1   **teaspoon Dijon mustard**
½   **teaspoon salt**
⅛   **teaspoon ground nutmeg**

Divide pastry into 6 equal portions. On a floured board, roll out each portion to fit a 4-inch tart pan about 1 inch deep. Line each pan with pastry; then, using a sharp knife or your fingers, trim or pinch off edges even with pan rim. Place pans on a large baking sheet; sprinkle cheese into pastry shells, dividing it equally among shells.

Preheat oven to 450°. Melt butter with tarragon in a wide frying pan over medium heat. Add watercress; stir just until coated with butter and slightly wilted (30 seconds to 1 minute).

Remove pan from heat and transfer watercress mixture to a blender or food processor; add eggs, half-and-half, mustard, salt, and nutmeg. Whirl until watercress is puréed. Pour purée evenly over cheese in pastry shells.

Bake for 10 minutes. Reduce oven heat to 350° and continue to bake until tarts are golden brown all over and a knife inserted in centers comes out clean (18 to 20 more minutes). Place on a rack and let cool for about 5 minutes, then carefully lift tarts out of pans and place on a serving plate. Makes 6.

Savory Fila Pastries

Dishes made with flaky, paper-thin fila look complex and impressive—but in fact, they're remarkably easy to put together. For tips on working with fila, see page 65.

Fila Chicken Packets

Boneless chicken breasts baked in crisp fila wrappers make an attractive company dish. The packets can be frozen for up to 1 month, then thawed in the refrigerator before baking.

- ¾ cup *each* chopped green onions (including tops) and mayonnaise
- 3 tablespoons lemon juice
- 3 cloves garlic, minced or pressed
- ¾ teaspoon dry tarragon
- ⅔ cup butter or margarine, melted
- 12 sheets fila (thawed if frozen)
- 3 whole chicken breasts (about 1 lb. *each*), skinned, boned, and split
  Salt and pepper
- 2 tablespoons grated Parmesan cheese

In a bowl, stir together onions, mayonnaise, lemon juice, 2 cloves of the garlic, and tarragon; set aside. Then, in another bowl, combine butter and remaining 1 clove garlic.

Preheat oven to 375°. Unroll fila and lay flat; cover with plastic wrap to prevent drying. For each packet, place one sheet of fila on a board and brush with about 2 teaspoons of the garlic butter. Place a second sheet of fila over the first; brush with 2 more teaspoons garlic butter. Sprinkle a chicken piece lightly with salt and pepper, then spread one side with about 1½ tablespoons of the mayonnaise mixture. Place chicken, mayonnaise side down, in upper right corner of fila. Spoon about 1½ more tablespoons mayonnaise mixture over chicken.

To wrap chicken, flip right corner of fila over chicken and roll once. Fold left corner over and roll again. Bring opposite (right) side of fila over packet, then roll all the way to lower left corner.

Place packets slightly apart in an ungreased shallow baking pan. Brush tops of packets with remaining garlic butter; sprinkle evenly with cheese. Bake until golden (20 to 25 minutes). Serve hot. Makes 6 servings.

Greens Pie

Greek *spanakopita* is a good vegetarian main dish; you might also serve it as an accompaniment to roast lamb or chicken.

- 1 to 1¼ pounds Swiss chard, rinsed well
- 1½ to 2 pounds spinach, rinsed well
  About ¼ pound parsley
- ¼ cup olive oil
- 6 to 8 green onions (including tops), thinly sliced
- 4 eggs
- ½ teaspoon *each* salt and pepper
- ⅛ teaspoon ground nutmeg
- 12 ounces feta cheese, crumbled (about 2½ cups)
- 10 sheets fila (thawed if frozen)
- ½ cup (¼ lb.) butter or margarine, melted

Remove and discard tough stems from chard; stack leaves, then cut crosswise into ¼-inch-wide slivers. Remove and discard spinach stems, stack leaves, and sliver as for chard. Discard parsley stems, then mince leaves. (You should have a total of about 4½ quarts prepared greens.)

Heat oil in a wide frying pan over medium heat. Add onions and stir until limp and bright green. Carefully mix in greens, turning just until coated with oil mixture and slightly softened. Turn greens into a colander; press to remove excess moisture. In a large bowl, beat eggs with salt, pepper, and nutmeg. Add greens and cheese and stir until evenly mixed.

Unroll fila, and lay flat; cover with plastic wrap to prevent drying. Generously brush bottom and sides of a 9 by 13-inch baking pan with some of the melted butter. Place one sheet of fila in pan, letting edges of fila extend over pan rim; brush with melted butter. Repeat layering and buttering with 4 more sheets of fila.

Spread greens mixture in pan, then fold overhanging fila over filling. Fold remaining 5 fila sheets to fit pan; place over greens, one at a time, brushing each with butter.

Brush top with any remaining butter. With a sharp knife, score top fila layers into 24 squares, making 3 lengthwise and 5 crosswise cuts. (At this point, you may cover and refrigerate for up to 24 hours.)

Preheat oven to 375°. Bake, uncovered, until pastry is crisp and well browned and filling is set (40 to 45 minutes). Serve hot or at room temperature; to serve, cut marked squares all the way through. Makes 24 pieces (10 to 12 servings).

Savory Fila Appetizer Pastries

1 Unroll stacked sheets of fila, taking care not to tear. Cut sheets in half crosswise, then cover with plastic wrap to prevent drying.

2 For logs, brush fila half sheets with butter; fold in half crosswise and brush again with butter. Place 1½ tablespoons filling along short end, fold in edges, and roll up.

3 For coils, brush fila half sheets with butter; fold in half lengthwise. Brush again with butter. Spoon 1½ tablespoons spinach filling along edge of dough; roll up, then coil.

4 For triangles, cut fila half sheets lengthwise into thirds; brush with butter. Fold corner over filling; continue folding like a flag.

Savory Fila Appetizer Pastries

(Pictured on facing page)

When you need appetizers for a big party or savory snacks to take on a picnic, consider this array of flaky fila tidbits. You can make them up to a month ahead and freeze; all can be baked directly from the freezer.

The total number of pastries you can make from this recipe depends on the brand of fila dough you buy. We used a 1-pound package that contained about 25 sheets, but number of sheets per pound (and their dimensions, as well) varies with the manufacturer. In any case, you'll get about three times as many cheese triangles as lamb logs and spinach coils.

Spicy Lamb Filling (recipe follows)
Spinach-Cheese Filling (recipe follows)
Feta Cheese Filling (recipe follows)
1 package (1 lb.) fila (thawed if frozen)
1 cup (½ lb.) butter or margarine, melted

Prepare fillings and set aside. Unroll fila and lay flat; cut sheets in half crosswise and cover with plastic wrap to prevent drying.

Use a third of the fila for each filling. Work with a half sheet of fila at a time; lightly brush with butter before filling.

Fill and shape pastries as directed below, then place shaped pastries about 1½ inches apart on greased baking sheets. Brush tops with butter and cover with plastic wrap while shaping remaining pastries.

To shape lamb logs (see photo 2 on the facing page), fold buttered half sheet of fila in half crosswise. Brush again with butter. Place 1½ tablespoons of the Spicy Lamb Filling along short end of each piece; fold in sides, then roll up dough jelly roll style.

To shape spinach coils (see photo 3 on the facing page), fold buttered half sheet of fila in half lengthwise; brush again with butter. Distribute 1½ tablespoons of the Spinach-Cheese Filling along long side of dough; roll up jelly roll style, then twist into a coil. Tuck end beneath coil.

To shape cheese triangles (see photo 4 on the facing page), cut buttered fila half sheet lengthwise into thirds. Place 1 tablespoon of the Feta Cheese Filling in upper corner of each strip and fold corner down over filling to make a triangle. Fold triangle over onto itself. Then continue folding triangle

from side to side all down length of strip, as if you were folding a flag.

(After shaping pastries, you may freeze them for up to 1 month. To freeze, place shaped pastries in freezer until firm; then carefully stack in a rigid container, placing foil between each layer of pastries. Do not thaw before baking.)

Preheat oven to 375°. Bake pastries until well browned and crisp (10 to 15 minutes; about 35 minutes if frozen). Serve hot; or let cool to room temperature, then serve. Makes about 16 *each* lamb logs and spinach coils, and about 48 cheese triangles.

Spicy Lamb Filling. Place a wide frying pan over medium heat; crumble in 1¼ pounds lean ground lamb. Add 1 large onion (chopped) and 2 cloves garlic (minced or pressed). Cook, stirring often, until onion is soft and meat is browned. Spoon off and discard any excess fat. Add ⅓ cup *each* catsup and chopped parsley; ½ cup dry red wine; 1 small can (8 oz.) stewed tomatoes; and ½ teaspoon *each* pepper and ground nutmeg.

Cook, stirring occasionally, for 10 minutes. Increase heat to high and continue to cook, stirring constantly, until almost all liquid has evaporated. Remove pan from heat and let filling cool for about 10 minutes.

If made ahead, cover and refrigerate for up to 2 days; bring to room temperature before using.

Spinach-Cheese Filling. Thaw 1 package (10 oz.) frozen chopped spinach; squeeze dry and set aside.

Heat 2 tablespoons olive oil in a wide frying pan over medium heat. Add 1 cup sliced green onions (including tops) and 2 cloves garlic (minced or pressed). Cook, stirring often, until onions are soft. Add spinach; cook, stirring, for 1 minute. Remove from heat and stir in 8 ounces ricotta cheese; 8 ounces feta cheese, crumbled (about 2 cups); 2 eggs (lightly beaten); 1 teaspoon oregano leaves; ¼ teaspoon *each* pepper and ground nutmeg; and ¼ cup *each* grated Parmesan cheese, fine dry bread crumbs, and chopped parsley.

If made ahead, cover and refrigerate for up to 2 days; bring to room temperature before using.

Feta Cheese Filling. In large bowl of an electric mixer, combine 8 ounces ricotta cheese; 8 ounces feta cheese, crumbled (about 2 cups); 1 small package (3 oz.) cream cheese (softened); 2 tablespoons all-purpose flour; 2 eggs; ½ teaspoon ground nutmeg; ¼ teaspoon white pepper; and ½ cup finely chopped parsley. Beat until mixture is well blended.

If made ahead, cover and refrigerate for up to 2 days; bring to room temperature before using.

Hearty Entrée Pies

There's something irresistibly homey about savory pastry-topped pies and flaky turnovers filled with meat or chicken.

Pizza Pot Pie

The popular flavors of pizza and its crust-enclosed cousin, calzone, are combined in this handsome deep-dish pie. It's good family fare, at home or on a picnic, and can be served hot or at room temperature. Accompany the pie with a green salad and red wine.

	Flaky Pastry for a double-crust 9-inch pie (page 7), made with ⅔ cup fat and 4 to 5 tablespoons water
1½	pounds mild Italian sausage, casings removed
3	cloves garlic, minced or pressed
1	teaspoon *each* fennel seeds and oregano leaves
1	teaspoon crushed dried hot red chiles
½	teaspoon pepper
3	pear-shaped tomatoes, seeded and chopped
2	cups (8 oz.) shredded mozzarella cheese
3	eggs, lightly beaten
¾	cup shredded or grated Parmesan cheese
¼	pound very thinly sliced prosciutto
1	pound ricotta cheese
12	to 15 large fresh basil leaves

Prepare Flaky Pastry for a double-crust 9-inch pie as directed on page 7, but reduce amount of fat to ⅔ cup and water to 4 to 5 tablespoons. Set aside.

Place a 10 to 12-inch frying pan over medium-high heat; crumble in sausage and cook, stirring, until meat loses its pink color (about 10 minutes). Add garlic, fennel seeds, oregano, chiles, pepper, and tomatoes. Continue to cook, stirring, until mixture boils (about 5 more minutes). Remove from heat; mix in mozzarella cheese, eggs, and ½ cup of the Parmesan cheese. Set aside and let cool slightly (or let cool completely, then cover and refrigerate for up to 24 hours).

On a lightly floured board, roll out half the pastry to an oval large enough to cover bottom and sides of a shallow 8 by 12-inch oval baking dish. Fit pastry into dish, letting edges extend over rim of dish. Spoon sausage mixture into pastry shell; cover with prosciutto. Dot ricotta over prosciutto, then spread as evenly as possible. Cover with basil leaves.

Preheat oven to 375°. Roll out remaining pastry and place on pie; trim, seal, and flute edges (see page 13). Pierce top in several places with a fork to allow steam to escape during baking.

Bake on lowest rack of oven until edges of pastry are browned (about 1 hour); about 10 minutes before pie is done, sprinkle with remaining ¼ cup Parmesan cheese. Serve hot or at room temperature. To serve, scoop each portion out of dish with a spoon. Makes 8 to 10 servings.

Chicken & Cheese Pastel

Pastry seasoned with chili powder encloses this Mexican-style supper pie, called a *pastel*. Team the pie with a salad of drained pickled beets and thinly sliced peeled jicama and oranges in vinaigrette dressing.

	Seasoned Pastry for a double-crust 9-inch pie (page 7), made with chili powder
2	cups (8 oz.) *each* shredded jack cheese and shredded mild Cheddar cheese
2	cups shredded cooked chicken
1	cup finely chopped cooked ham
⅓	cup *each* thinly sliced green onions (including tops) and chopped fresh cilantro (coriander)
1	large can (7 oz.) diced green chiles, drained
½	teaspoon *each* salt and ground cumin
¼	teaspoon ground red pepper (cayenne)
1	egg yolk beaten with 1 teaspoon water
1	tablespoon sesame seeds

Preheat oven to 425°. Roll out a little more than half the pastry and line a 9-inch pie pan as directed on page 12.

In a medium-size bowl, mix cheeses, chicken, ham, onions, cilantro, chiles, salt, cumin, and pepper; mound in pastry shell.

Roll out remaining pastry and place on pie; trim, seal, and flute edges (see page 13). Brush with egg yolk mixture, then pierce top with a fork in several places. Sprinkle with sesame seeds.

Bake on lowest rack of oven until well browned (30 to 35 minutes). Let pie stand for 5 minutes before cutting into wedges. Serve hot. Makes 6 servings.

Beef & Spinach Supper Pie

A crunchy oatmeal pastry enhances this savory entrée made with versatile ground beef; it's topped with sliced tomatoes and melted cheese. Both pastry and filling can be made ahead and refrigerated —separately—for up to a day.

As a variation, you might substitute an equal weight of mild Italian sausage (casings removed, crumbled) for the ground beef and replace the Cheddar cheese with jack or fontina. If you wish, use a sweet red bell pepper in place of the green pepper. As a side dish, serve cut Italian green beans, cooked tender-crisp.

> Oatmeal Pastry for a single-crust 9-inch pie (page 7)
> 1 tablespoon salad oil
> 1 medium-size onion, finely chopped
> 1 medium-size green bell pepper, seeded and chopped
> 1 clove garlic, minced or pressed
> 1 pound lean ground beef
> 1 teaspoon *each* salt and oregano leaves
> ½ teaspoon *each* dry basil and marjoram leaves
> ¼ teaspoon pepper
> ¼ cup catsup
> 1 package (10 oz.) frozen chopped spinach, thawed
> 3 eggs, lightly beaten
> 2 cups (8 oz.) shredded sharp Cheddar cheese
> 1 large firm-ripe tomato, sliced

Preheat oven to 400°. Roll out pastry and line a 9-inch pie pan as directed on page 12.

Heat oil in a wide frying pan over medium heat. Add onion, bell pepper, and garlic; cook, stirring often, until onion is soft but not browned (4 to 6 minutes). Crumble beef into pan; cook, stirring, until meat loses its pink color. Spoon off and discard any excess fat. Mix in salt, oregano, basil, marjoram, pepper, and catsup.

Drain spinach, pressing out excess moisture. Stir into meat mixture; remove from heat. Let cool slightly, then blend in eggs and 1 cup of the cheese.

Spoon filling into pastry shell. Bake on lowest rack of oven until filling is just set in center (about 30 minutes). Remove from oven and arrange tomato slices attractively over top; sprinkle evenly with remaining 1 cup cheese. Return to oven and continue to bake until cheese is melted (about 5 more minutes). Let stand for 5 minutes before cutting into wedges. Makes 4 to 6 servings.

Crunchy Beef Turnovers

These turnovers are a good choice for a make-ahead supper, since they can wait in the refrigerator for up to a day before baking. Their appetizing appearance and crunch comes from a coating of crushed tortilla chips; if you wish, you can use nacho or cheese-flavored chips for a nippier-tasting crust. Accompany the turnovers with icy cold beer and a salad of soft lettuce in an oil and vinegar dressing. Fruit of the season makes a light, refreshing dessert.

> 1 tablespoon salad oil
> 1 medium-size onion, finely chopped
> ½ pound lean ground beef
> 1 clove garlic, minced or pressed
> 1 beef bouillon cube, crushed
> 2 teaspoons chili powder
> 1 teaspoon curry powder
> 1 green bell pepper, seeded and chopped
> 1 large tart green apple (unpeeled), cored and chopped
> 1 cup (4 oz.) shredded jack or Cheddar cheese
> Salt
> Flaky Pastry for a double-crust 9-inch pie (page 7)
> 1 ounce tortilla chips, crushed to make ¼ cup

Heat oil in a medium-size frying pan over medium-high heat. Add onion and crumble in beef; cook, stirring, until meat loses its pink color. Spoon off and discard any excess fat. Mix in garlic, bouillon cube, chili powder, and curry powder. Stir in bell pepper and apple; remove from heat. Mix in cheese, then season to taste with salt.

On a floured pastry cloth or board, roll out half the pastry to a 10-inch circle. Spread half the crushed tortilla chips on a flat surface; invert pastry onto chips and press lightly to embed chips in dough. Place pastry circle, chip side down, on an ungreased baking sheet. Spoon half the beef mixture over half the circle, spreading to within 1 inch of edges. Carefully fold other half of pastry over filling; pinch edges to seal.

Repeat with remaining pastry, chips, and beef mixture to make a second turnover. Sprinkle evenly with any remaining chips, pressing in lightly. (At this point, you may cover turnovers and refrigerate for up to 24 hours.)

Preheat oven to 425°. Bake turnovers, uncovered, until edges are crisp and browned (25 to 30 minutes; about 35 minutes if refrigerated). Slide onto a platter to serve. Makes 2 turnovers (4 to 6 servings *total*).

Puff Pastry Boxes

Artfully shaped puff pastry "boxes" make striking looking edible containers for creamy seafood or poultry.

When working with puff pastry, take care to handle it as little and as lightly as possible and to keep it cool. These precautions help produce finished pastry that's both tender and puffed to its maximum volume.

Scallops & Spinach in Puff Pastry

(Pictured on facing page)

This elegant main dish requires last-minute attention, but it's not difficult to complete if you have all the elements prepared and ready to cook.

The puff pastry cases for this dish are entrée-size rectangles. If you would prefer a smaller serving—for a first course—you can cut the same amount of puff pastry into squares instead; make them about 2½ inches on each side. Assemble and bake the squares as directed for the larger rectangles. Use the spinach-scallop filling below— or substitute your favorite sautéed mushrooms, or even tiny snails in herbed garlic butter.

- 1 **sheet (half of a 17¼-oz. package) frozen puff pastry**
- 1 **egg beaten with 1 teaspoon water**
  About ½ pound spinach
- ½ **cup dry white wine**
- 2 **tablespoons lemon juice**
- ¼ **teaspoon dry tarragon**
- 1 **shallot, finely chopped (about 2 tablespoons)**
- 1 **pound small bay scallops, rinsed and drained (or large scallops, cut into ¼-inch-thick slices)**
- ½ **cup whipping cream**
- 1 **teaspoon Dijon mustard**
- ¼ **cup cold butter or margarine, cut into 2 pieces**

Thaw pastry at room temperature for 20 minutes. Unfold and place on a lightly floured board. Using a floured sharp knife or pastry wheel, cut pastry into 8 equal-size rectangles—each about 2¼ by 5 inches. Cut centers from 4 of the rectangles, making ½-inch-wide "frames" (see photo 1 on the facing page).

Transfer the 4 uncut (whole) rectangles to an ungreased large baking sheet; lightly brush edges with cold water. Carefully lift "frames" from remaining 4 rectangles, using a narrow metal spatula; place a "frame" on each uncut rectangle, pressing down lightly to seal. Transfer the 4 cut-out centers to baking sheet. Refrigerate for at least 30 minutes or up to 2 hours.

Preheat oven to 400°. Brush cut-out centers and "frames" with egg mixture, taking care not to let any of it drip down sides (this would cause pastry to stick to baking sheet). Pierce cut-out centers with a fork to make a decorative pattern.

Bake until centers are browned (about 15 minutes); transfer them to a rack. Return baking sheet to oven and continue to bake until pastry boxes are golden brown (5 to 10 more minutes). Transfer to a rack and let cool. Then, using a fork, remove and discard any soft dough from centers of boxes. Let baked centers and boxes stand, uncovered, for up to 2 hours.

Rinse spinach well; drain. Remove and discard stems, then place leaves with the water that clings to them in a 2½ to 3-quart pan. Cover and set aside (moisture clinging to leaves will be sufficient cooking liquid).

Preheat oven to 350°. Place baked, cooled pastry boxes and centers on a baking sheet; set aside.

In a 10 to 12-inch frying pan, combine wine, lemon juice, tarragon, and shallot. Bring to a boil over medium-high heat. Add scallops and cook, uncovered, turning often with a wide spatula, until opaque throughout (2 to 3 minutes). Remove pan from heat; lift out scallops with a slotted spoon and set aside. Reserve poaching liquid in pan to use in sauce.

Place pastry in oven and reheat for about 5 minutes. Place pan of spinach over medium-high heat; cook, covered, stirring once or twice, just until leaves are limp and bright green (2 to 3 minutes). Remove from heat and keep warm.

Add cream and mustard to scallop cooking liquid in frying pan. Bring to a boil over high heat; boil, uncovered, stirring often, until large, shiny bubbles form and liquid is reduced to about ½ cup. Reduce heat to low; stir in butter, one piece at a time, stirring constantly to blend in butter as it melts (butter thickens sauce). Add scallops and stir gently until heated through.

To serve, place one puff pastry box on each of 4 warm dinner plates. Lift spinach leaves from pan with a fork; line each box with a few leaves. Spoon in scallops, letting some of the mixture drizzle onto plate around pastry. Perch a pastry center at a jaunty angle on one side of box. Serve hot. Makes 4 servings.

Scallops & Spinach in Puff Pastry

1 Cut thawed puff pastry into 8 rectangles; cut out centers of 4 of them to make "frames." Handle lightly so baked pastry will be light and tender.

2 Transfer uncut rectangles and cut-out centers to a baking sheet with a spatula. Moisten edges of uncut rectangles, then position "frames" over them. Refrigerate pastry.

3 Scallops poaching liquid is reduced, then thickened with butter to make a creamy sauce. Add chilled butter in 2 chunks, stirring constantly to mix it in smoothly.

4 Lightly cooked spinach lines baked puff pastry cases. Have scallops in creamy sauce ready to spoon over spinach to complete the dish.

Hors d'Oeuvre Pastries

Flaky pastry or puff pastry makes a crisp, rich base for some of the most appealing hot hors d'oeuvres or appetizers you can make. All these tidbits can be made ahead and either frozen or refrigerated until ready to bake or reheat.

Curried Chicken Barquettes

The name *barquette*—"small boat" in French—is appropriate for these small tarts. You bake the rich pastry shells empty, then spoon in a savory filling. Our creamy chicken, mushroom, or shrimp barquettes are a good choice for appetizers or for a light lunch. To make them, you'll need tart pans measuring about 2 by 4½ inches.

> **Flaky Butter Pastry for a single-crust 9-inch pie (page 7)**
> 2 tablespoons butter or margarine
> 2 green onions (including tops), thinly sliced
> 1 clove garlic, minced or pressed
> 2 tablespoons all-purpose flour
> 1¼ teaspoons curry powder
> ¼ teaspoon salt
> 1 cup regular-strength chicken broth
> 1½ cups finely chopped cooked chicken
> 2 to 3 tablespoons chopped chutney

On a floured board, roll out pastry to a thickness of about ¹⁄₁₆ inch. To make shells, invert an oval tart pan (about 2 by 4½ inches) onto pastry; cut around pan with a knife, making an oval about ½ inch larger all around than pan. Re-roll scraps and cut again to make a total of 12 to 15 ovals. Press ovals lightly over bottom and up sides of tart pans, pinching off any pastry that extends over edges. Pierce each pastry shell in several places with a fork.

Preheat oven to 400°. Place pans on a large baking sheet; bake until pastry is lightly browned (12 to 15 minutes). Place pans on a rack and let cool; then carefully remove shells from pans and arrange in a single layer in a shallow rimmed baking pan. If made ahead, cover and freeze for up to 2 weeks.

Melt butter in a medium-size pan over medium heat. Add onions; cook, stirring occasionally, until limp and bright green. Mix in garlic, flour, curry powder, and salt; cook until bubbly. Remove from heat and gradually blend in broth. Cook, stirring, until sauce boils and thickens. Mix in chicken.

Spoon hot chicken filling into pastry shells. Top each barquette with about ½ teaspoon chutney. To serve at once, broil about 4 inches below heat until filling is bubbly (2 to 3 minutes). Or, if made ahead, cover and refrigerate for up to 24 hours. To serve, heat uncovered, in a 350° oven until heated through (5 to 10 minutes). Makes 12 to 15.

Creamy Mushroom Barquettes

Prepare pastry shells as directed for **Curried Chicken Barquettes.** For the filling, melt ¼ cup **butter** or margarine in a wide frying pan over medium-high heat. Add ½ pound **mushrooms,** finely chopped, 1 **shallot,** finely chopped (about 2 tablespoons), and ½ cup very finely chopped **cooked ham.** Cook, stirring often, until liquid has evaporated and mushrooms are lightly browned. Stir in 1 tablespoon **lemon juice,** 1 teaspoon **Dijon mustard,** ¼ teaspoon **dry tarragon,** ⅛ teaspoon **white pepper,** and ½ cup **whipping cream.** Continue to cook, stirring often, until sauce is thickened and reduced to about 1½ cups.

Spoon mushroom sauce evenly into pastry shells; top each barquette with about 1 teaspoon finely shredded **Gruyère or Swiss cheese** (you'll need about ⅓ cup *total*). Broil or bake as directed for **Curried Chicken Barquettes.**

Glazed Shrimp Barquettes

Prepare pastry shells as directed for **Curried Chicken Barquettes.** For the filling, stir together ½ pound **small cooked shrimp,** 2 tablespoons **mayonnaise,** 1 teaspoon **Dijon mustard,** and 2 tablespoons finely chopped **parsley** until well combined.

Spoon shrimp filling evenly into pastry shells; top each barquette with 1 scant tablespoon finely shredded **jack cheese** (you'll need about ¾ cup *total*). Broil or bake as directed for **Curried Chicken Barquettes.**

Tiny Ham & Cheese Tarts

Serve these French tidbits with wine-based apéritifs or champagne.

    1 sheet (half of a 17¼-oz. package) frozen
       puff pastry
    ¼ cup very finely chopped
       cooked ham
    ½ cup finely shredded Gruyère or Swiss
       cheese

Thaw puff pastry at room temperature for 20 minutes. Unfold. On a lightly floured board, roll out pastry to make an 11-inch square. Cut pastry into 2-inch circles; re-roll scraps and cut again. Fit each circle lightly into bottom and part way up sides of a 1¾-inch muffin cup (measured across the top).

Fill each pastry shell with a rounded ¼ teaspoon ham and a rounded ½ teaspoon cheese. Refrigerate for at least 30 minutes or up to 2 hours. Preheat oven to 450°. Bake tarts until golden brown (12 to 15 minutes). Serve hot. Makes about 36.

Cheese Twists

Swiss cheese makes these a hit with salad.

    1 sheet (half of a 17¼-oz. package) frozen
       puff pastry
    1 egg beaten with 1 teaspoon water
    ½ cup finely shredded Swiss or Gruyère
       cheese

Thaw puff pastry at room temperature for 20 minutes. Unfold. On a lightly floured board, roll out pastry to make a 16-inch square. Brush with just enough of the egg mixture to coat evenly; sprinkle evenly with cheese. Fold in half, making an 8 by 16-inch rectangle. Cut in half lengthwise; then cut crosswise into ½-inch-wide, 4-inch-long strips. Hold each strip at ends and twist in opposite directions.

Place twists about ½ inch apart on greased baking sheets. Refrigerate for at least 30 minutes or up to 2 hours. Preheat oven to 425°. Brush pastry twists with some of the remaining egg mixture; bake until twists are golden brown (10 to 12 minutes). Serve at once. Makes 64.

Herbed Cheese Appetizer Wedges

There's a savory center in every bite of these hot, pastry-enclosed morsels. For the filling, take your choice of two cheeses—French-style cream cheese flavored with herbs and garlic, or a blue-veined type such as Roquefort or Gorgonzola.

    1 sheet (half of a 17¼-oz. package) frozen
       puff pastry
    4 ounces cream cheese flavored with
       herbs and garlic
    1 egg, separated
    2 tablespoons whipping cream

Thaw puff pastry at room temperature for 20 minutes. Unfold. On a lightly floured board, roll out pastry to make an 11-inch square; cut a 10-inch circle from center. Use circle to line a 9-inch tart pan with a removable bottom or a 9-inch spring-form pan; let edges of pastry extend up against sides of pan.

In a bowl, beat cheese, egg yolk, and cream until blended. Spread over pastry circle in pan; fold pastry edges down to cover edges of filling. Reshape pastry trimmings into a ball and roll out to a thin 9-inch circle. Moisten edges of pastry in pan with cold water. Place 9-inch pastry circle over filling, pressing edges to seal.

Refrigerate for at least 30 minutes or up to 2 hours. Preheat oven to 425°. Lightly beat egg white with 1 teaspoon water; brush over pastry. With a small, sharp knife, lightly score top in a decorative pattern (a checkerboard design or curving lines radiating from center).

Bake until pastry is well browned (20 to 25 minutes). Remove sides of pan, cut pastry into wedges, and serve hot. Makes 6 to 8 servings.

Blue Cheese Appetizer Wedges

Prepare puff pastry as directed for **Herbed Cheese Appetizer Wedges**. Omit cream cheese. For the filling, crumble 4 ounces **blue-veined cheese** (you'll have about 1 cup). Sprinkle cheese over pastry in tart pan. Beat 1 **egg yolk** with ¼ cup **whipping cream** or sour cream; drizzle evenly over cheese. Continue as for **Herbed Cheese Appetizer Wedges**.

Index

Coconut Tart (*recipe on page 47*)

Index **95**

Metric Conversion Table

To change	To	Multiply by
ounces (oz.)	grams (g)	28
pounds (lbs.)	kilograms (kg)	0.45
teaspoons	milliliters (ml)	5
tablespoons	milliliters (ml)	15
fluid ounces (fl. oz.)	milliliters (ml)	30
cups	liters (l)	0.24
pints (pt.)	liters (l)	0.47
quarts (qt.)	liters (l)	0.95
gallons (gal.)	liters (l)	3.8
Fahrenheit temperature (°F)	Celsius temperature (°C)	$\frac{5}{9}$ after subtracting 32